OECD Economic Surveys: Iceland 2015

This document and any map included herein are without prejudice to the status of or sovereignty over any territory, to the delimitation of international frontiers and boundaries and to the name of any territory, city or area.

Please cite this publication as:
OECD (2015), *OECD Economic Surveys: Iceland 2015*, OECD Publishing, Paris.
http://dx.doi.org/10.1787/eco_surveys-isl-2015-en

ISBN 978-92-64-24041-4 (print)
ISBN 978-92-64-24049-0 (PDF)
ISBN 978-92-64-24051-3 (epub)

Series: OECD Economic Surveys
ISSN 0376-6438 (print)
ISSN 1609-7513 (online)

OECD Economic Surveys: Iceland
ISSN 1995-3240 (print)
ISSN 1999-0308 (online)

The statistical data for Israel are supplied by and under the responsibility of the relevant Israeli authorities. The use of such data by the OECD is without prejudice to the status of the Golan Heights, East Jerusalem and Israeli settlements in the West Bank under the terms of international law.

Photo credits: Cover © marchello/Shutterstock.com

Corrigenda to OECD publications may be found on line at: *www.oecd.org/about/publishing/corrigenda.htm*.

Table of contents

Thematic chapters

Boxes

Tables

Figures

This Survey is published on the responsibility of the Economic and Development Review Committee of the OECD, which is charged with the examination of the economic situation of member countries.

The Economic situation and policies of Iceland were reviewed by the Committee on 23 June 2015. The draft was revised in the light of the discussion and given final approval as the agreed report of the whole Committee on 15 July 2015.

The Secretariat's draft report was prepared for the Committee by Douglas Sutherland and Jonathan Millar under the supervision of Patrick Lenain. Damien Azzopardi and Valery Dugain provided the statistical research assistance, and Brigitte Beyeler provided the administrative support. The Survey also benefited from contributions by Gunnar Haraldsson.

The previous Survey of Iceland was issued in June 2013

BASIC STATISTICS OF ICELAND, 2014

(Numbers in parentheses refer to the OECD average)*

LAND, PEOPLE AND ELECTORAL CYCLE					
Population (million)	0.3		Population density per km²	3.2	(34.9)
Under 15 (%)	20.6	(18.2)	Life expectancy (years, 2012)	83.0	(80.2)
Over 65 (%)	13.2	(16.0)	Men	81.6	(77.5)
Foreign-born (%, 2012)	11.1		Women	84.3	(82.9)
Latest 5-year average growth (%)	0.4	(0.6)	Latest general election	April 2013	
ECONOMY					
Gross domestic product (GDP)			Value added shares (%, 2013)		
In current prices (billion USD)	17.1		Primary sector	6.8	(2.5)
In current prices (billion ISK)	1 993		Industry including construction	23.4	(26.6)
Latest 5-year average real growth (%)	1.2	(1.9)	Services	69.7	(70.7)
Per capita (000 USD PPP)	44.7	(39.1)			
GENERAL GOVERNMENT Per cent of GDP					
Expenditure, 2014	45.4	(41.9)	Gross financial debt, 2014	85.3	(112.1)
Revenue, 2014	45.3	(38.0)	Net financial debt, 2014	26.0	(69.0)
EXTERNAL ACCOUNTS					
Exchange rate (ISK per USD)	116.6		Main exports (% of total merchandise exports)		
PPP exchange rate (USA = 1)	137.1		Manufactured goods	42.0	
In per cent of GDP			Food and live animals	41.8	
Exports of goods and services	53.5	(49.2)	Machinery and transport equipment	5.8	
Imports of goods and services	47.1	(46.0)	Main imports (% of total merchandise imports)		
Current account balance	3.6	(-0.1)	Machinery and transport equipment	31.1	
Net international investment position	-361.0		Mineral fuels, lubricants and related materials	17.2	
			Crude materials, inedible, except fuels	10.9	
LABOUR MARKET, SKILLS AND INNOVATION					
Employment rate for 15-64 year-olds (%)	81.6	(65.7)	Unemployment rate, Labour Force Survey (age 15 and over) (%)	4.9	(7.3)
Men	84.0	(73.6)	Youth (age 15-24, %)	9.8	(15.0)
Women	79.3	(57.9)	Long-term unemployed (1 year and over, %, 2013)	1.1	(2.7)
Participation rate for 15-64 year-olds (%, 2013)	86.6	(71.1)	Tertiary educational attainment 25-64 year-olds (%, 2013)	36.1	(33.3)
Average hours worked per year (2013)	1 704	(1 771)	Gross domestic expenditure on R&D (% of GDP, 2013)	2.5	(2.4)
ENVIRONMENT					
Total primary energy supply per capita (toe, 2013)	16.8	(4.2)	CO_2 emissions from fuel combustion per capita (tonnes, 2012)	5.8	(9.7)
Renewables (%, 2013)	89.0	(8.8)	Municipal waste per capita (tonnes, 2013)	0.3	(0.5)
Fine particulate matter concentration (urban, PM10, µg/m³, 2011)	17.7	(28.0)			
SOCIETY					
Income inequality (Gini coefficient, 2012)	0.257	(0.308)	Education outcomes (PISA score, 2012)		
Relative poverty rate (% below half of median income 2012)	6.3	(10.9)	Reading	483	(496)
Median equivalised household income (000 USD PPP, 2010)	23.2	(20.4)	Mathematics	493	(494)
Public and private spending (% of GDP)			Science	478	(501)
Health care (2012)	9.0	(9.2)	Share of women in parliament (%, May 2015)	41.3	(27.0)
Pensions (2011)	2.6	(8.7)	Net official development assistance (% of GNI)	0.21	(0.36)
Education (primary, secondary, post sec. non tertiary, 2011)	4.9	(3.9)			

Better life index: *www.oecdbetterlifeindex.org*

* Where the OECD aggregate is not provided in the source database, a simple OECD average of latest available data is calculated where data exist for at least 29 member countries.

Source: Calculations based on data extracted from the databases of the following organisations: OECD, International Energy Agency, World Bank, International Monetary Fund and Inter-Parliamentary Union.

Executive summary

- *Main findings*
- *Key recommendations*

Main findings

Iceland's economic prospects are good, but capital controls and wage increases are key challenges

Output has recovered

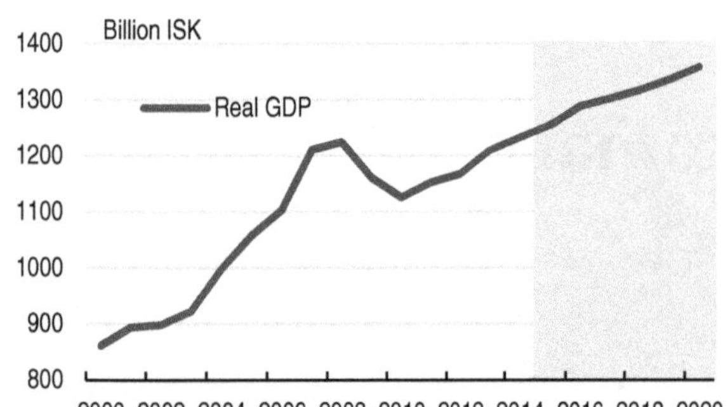

Source: OECD Economic Outlook 97 database and long term baseline.

StatLink http://dx.doi.org/10.1787/888933258386

Iceland has entered its 5th year of economic recovery and prospects are for continuing growth. Progress has been made on many fronts: inflation has come down, external imbalances have narrowed, public debt is falling, full employment has been restored and fewer families are facing financial distress. Lifting the capital controls introduced in 2008 in an orderly way is a challenge due to the complexity of the problem and the size of potential capital outflows. Large wage increases awarded during the recent collective bargaining round that are well in excess of productivity will require growth-weakening monetary tightening.

Fiscal policy has become more sustainable, but contingent liabilities remain a risk

The budget deficit has been eliminated

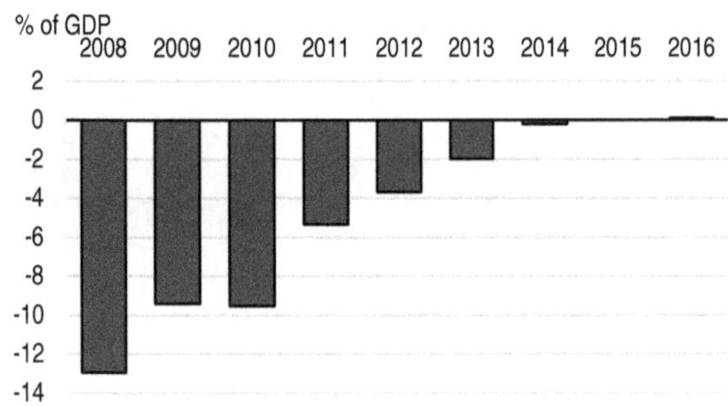

Source: OECD Economic Outlook 97 database.

StatLink http://dx.doi.org/10.1787/888933258394

Iceland has considerably improved its fiscal position. A budget surplus is about to be achieved and public debt has been lowered. Long-term projections suggest that fiscal policy had been on track to achieve sustainability before subsequent changes were made to secure wage settlements. The simulations also show that it would not take much to derail fiscal policy. In addition, spending pressures, notably future pension entitlements, remain a risk and contingent liabilities, such as the HFF guarantee, could have severe consequences. Staying the fiscal course by bringing down public debt levels further is therefore important to reap the gains of past efforts.

Barriers to entrepreneurship, lack of competition and weaknesses in education undermine productivity

Barriers to entrepreneurship are high

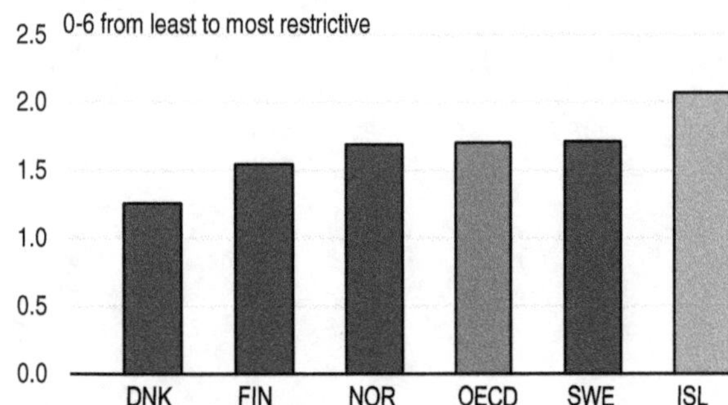

Source: OECD, Product Market Regulation indicators database.

StatLink http://dx.doi.org/10.1787/888933258402

Despite the recovery, income per capita remains lower than in other Nordic countries and near the OECD average, reflecting weaker productivity. While Iceland has a business-friendly environment, it can be difficult for new firms to enter markets, thus deterring innovation. Due to the small size of the economy, ensuring competition can be a challenge. Also undermining productivity are low skills in some of the labour force due to high drop-out rates from upper-secondary school.

Key recommendations

Lifting capital controls while preserving stability

- Progress is needed in lifting Iceland's capital controls and the current plan is a welcome step in this direction. Maintaining a robust macroeconomic stability framework will help avoid a disorderly outcome.
- Monetary policy needs to raise interest rates to ensure that a wage-price spiral does not develop, as already stated by the Monetary Policy Committee. The focus should remain on low and stable inflation over the medium term, while allowing the exchange rate to float apart from limited interventions to smooth erratic fluctuations.
- To protect macroeconomic stability the central bank should remain independent from political interference. The monetary policy committee introduced in 2009 should be retained.
- Strengthen the macro-prudential policy framework, incorporating tools to address large swings in capital flows unrelated to fundamentals, while respecting international commitments.
- To protect the economy from unavoidable shocks and reinforce confidence, buffers should be built up including ample fiscal space, foreign exchange reserves and bank capital and liquidity.
- Reforms to current labour market institutions are needed, including giving the state mediator more resources and power to arbitrate in favour of realistic wage agreements.

Securing fiscal sustainability

- Pass and implement the Organic Budget Law, including enacting the balanced budget rules and establishing an independent Fiscal Council to assess progress towards sustainability.
- Use windfall gains and one-off revenues to pay down debt, including any proceeds from lifting the capital controls.
- Avoid accumulating further contingent liabilities, including by closing the Housing Financing Fund (HFF).
- Further shift tax revenue from income taxes to VAT, while preserving equity.

Setting the course for productivity growth

- Adopt an ongoing productivity agenda, including following up on the priorities identified by the recent growth forum.
- Lower barriers to entry including by removing legal barriers to entry in particular sectors.
- Support innovation, including by encouraging links with universities. Ease funding access, notably with public investment funds that can finance firm expansion. Evaluate support measures.
- Toughen competition policy implementation to ensure that abuse of dominant position or cartel/tacit collusion does not stifle competition. Use the OECD's Competition Assessment Toolkit to refine law and enforcement.

Assessment and recommendations

- *The recovery from the crisis is well underway*
- *Lifting capital controls while preserving financial stability*
- *Securing long-term fiscal sustainability*
- *Supporting long-term productivity growth*

Iceland's small and open economy was severely hit by the crisis in October 2008 when its three major banks collapsed and the government lost access to international capital markets. The stabilisation programme conducted with international support was successfully completed in 2011 and economic activity has recovered steadily, returning to its pre-crisis level earlier than in euro-crisis countries (Figure 1). There are other signs of normalisation, such as lower inflation, falling unemployment, improved public finances and stronger household balance sheets.

Nevertheless, critical challenges inherited from the crisis– especially capital controls, and a heavy debt service burden – need to be addressed. A further set of challenges lies in managing wage pressures and in boosting long-term growth. Against this background the present economic survey identifies the following policy priorities:

- Unwinding capital controls
- Reforming the wage bargaining system
- Boosting productivity

Figure 1. **Output is recovering comparatively strongly**

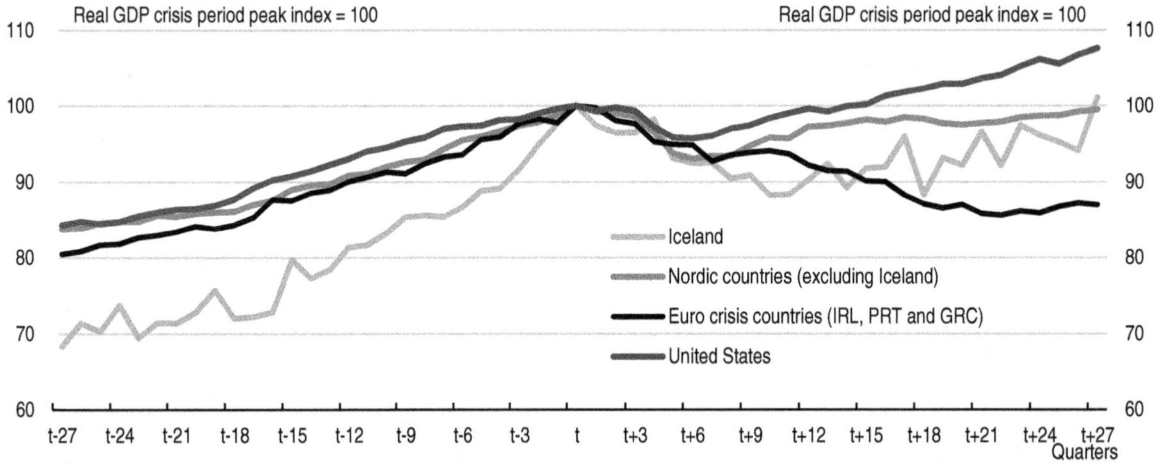

Note: Peak quarter is 2007Q4 for the Nordic countries and Ireland, 2008Q1 for Portugal, 2007Q2 for Greece and 2008Q2 for the United States.
Source: OECD, Analytical database.

StatLink http://dx.doi.org/10.1787/888933258411

The recovery from the crisis is well underway

Iceland has enjoyed a steady economic recovery, with consumer spending rising strongly. Business fixed investment has also recovered, but insufficiently to prevent the capital stock eroding (Figure 2). There is scope for investment to pick up (Lewis *et al.*, 2014) and new projects in the ferrosilicon sector are about to get underway. Public investment has been boosted in the 2015 budget, mainly in transportation projects.

In comparison with the past, considerable progress was made in 2014 and early 2015 in bringing down inflation (Figure 3, Panel B). Annual consumer price inflation has dipped

Figure 2. **Investment slumped after the crisis**

Residential, government, business investment and capital stock
Investment as % of GDP; Capital stock as % GDP

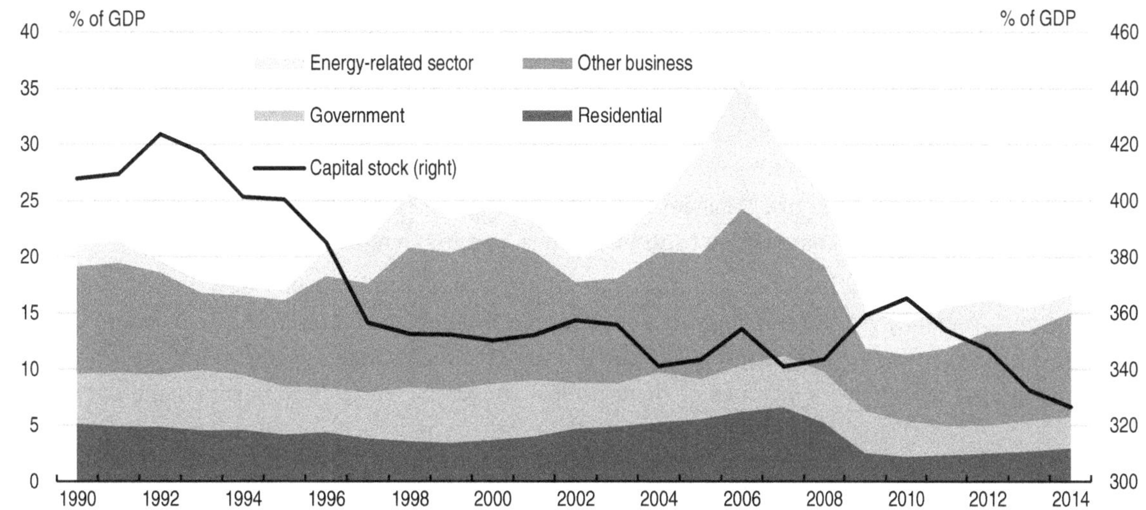

Source: OECD, Analytical database.

StatLink http://dx.doi.org/10.1787/888933258427

Figure 3. **Wage and price inflation**

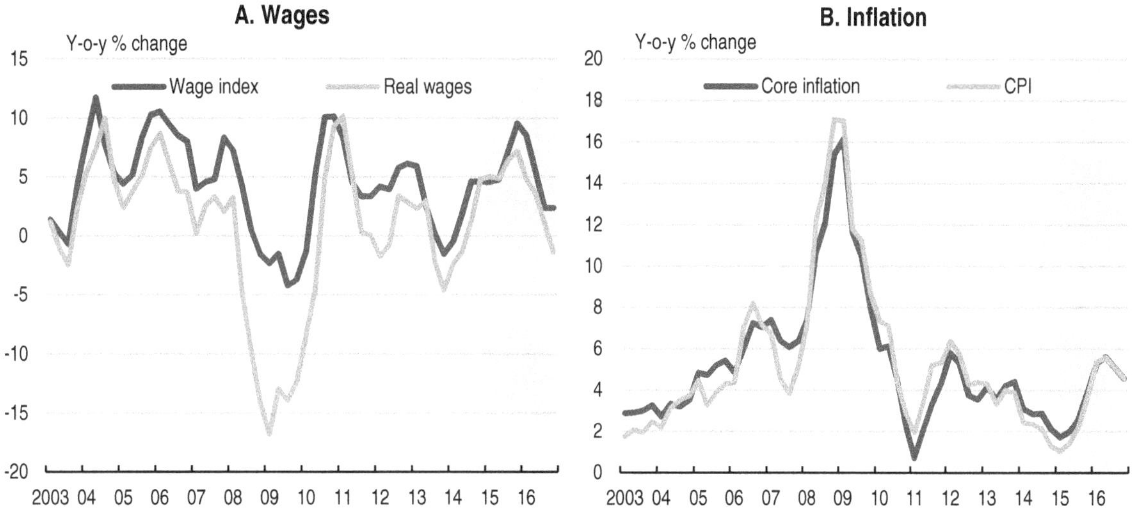

Note: The projections assume interest rates hikes and monetary policy credibility facilitating inflation moving back to target.
Source: OECD, Analytical database, Central Bank of Iceland and Statistics Iceland.

StatLink http://dx.doi.org/10.1787/888933258432

below the Central Bank's inflation target. The cost of housing has recently been the most dynamic component of the consumer price index, reflecting higher imputed rents in the greater Reykjavik area. However, recent wage settlements will push up inflation in the short term and high inflation may become entrenched without an adequate policy response.

The substantial depreciation of the króna from its pre-crisis level went a long way towards rebalancing the economy and helping the recovery, and more recently the large fall in oil prices and rise of marine product prices have improved the terms of trade and helped to reduce external imbalances (Figure 4, panel C). Exports of goods have also changed, with less reliance on the traditional exports of fish and aluminium and more on services, notably related to the tourism boom.

The labour market has improved considerably. Job gains have been large, especially in the tourism sector, and the unemployment rate dropped sharply (Figure 4, Panel A and B). Long-term unemployment remains somewhat higher than before the crisis, but has been steadily declining. With labour demand remaining strong, tensions in the labour market have intensified, notwithstanding a pickup in the immigration of workers, pushing real wages back towards their pre-crisis level (Figure 3, Panel A). Furthermore, large settlements in the recent collective bargaining round will raise nominal wages substantially.

The recovery of the labour market has helped households to pay down their debt (Figure 4, panel D). Additional support to household finance has come from the recovery in asset prices, rulings by the Supreme Court that certain loans indexed to foreign currency were illegal, and from a number of government programmes to reduce mortgage debt.

Figure 4. **The economy is normalising**

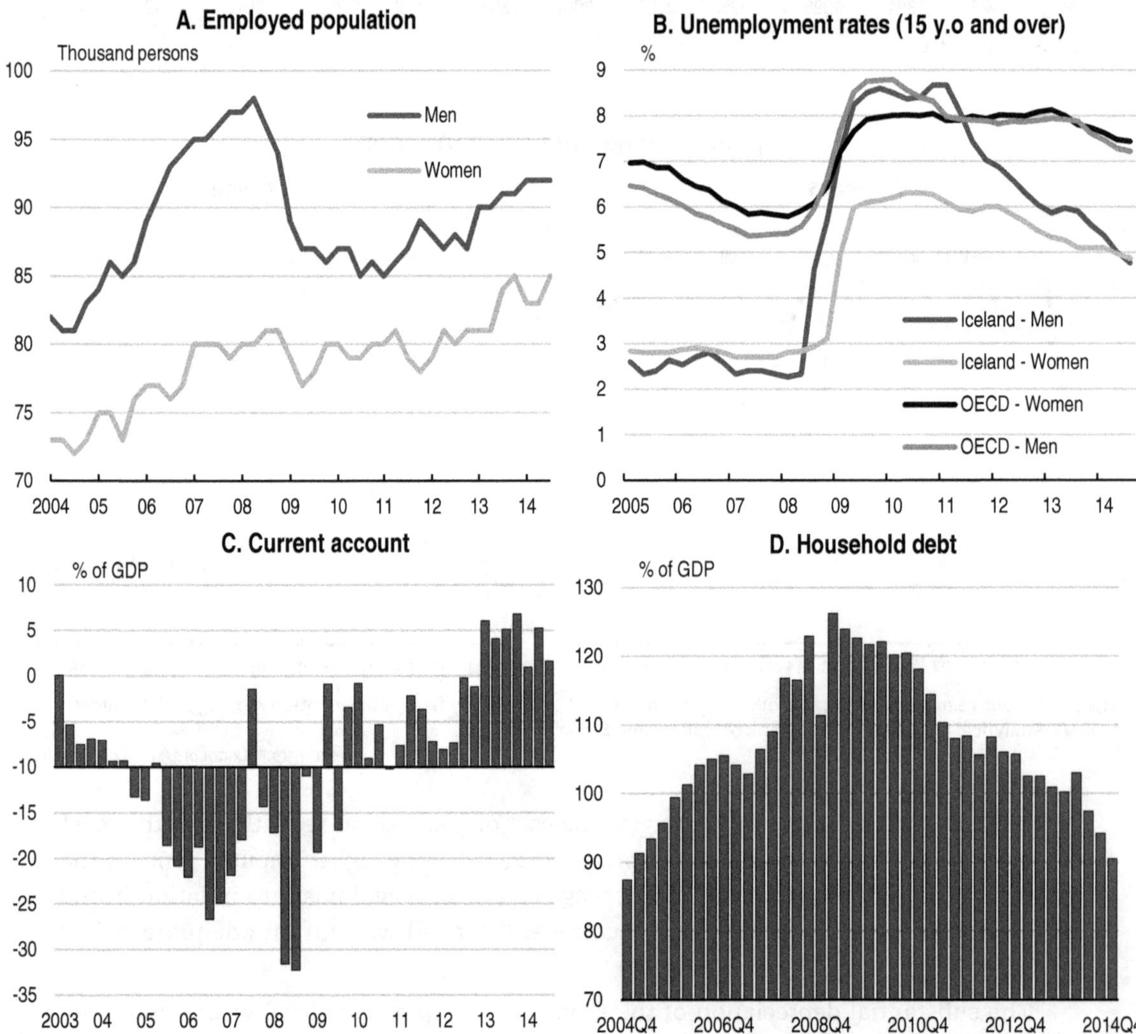

Source: OECD, Labour Force Statistics and Analytical databases, Central Bank of Iceland, Statistics Iceland.

StatLink http://dx.doi.org/10.1787/888933258443

These include the current government's programme to reduce mortgage debt by around 8% of household financial liabilities (relative to the end of 2013), which will be largely implemented in 2015 (Central Bank of Iceland, 2014). Healthier household balance sheets will further boost consumer spending.

Near-term economic prospects are good (Table 1). Lower energy prices, improved household balance sheets, higher business investment, less fiscal drag, monetary support and healthier export markets are all projected to sustain real GDP growth of over 4% a year in 2015 and around 3% in 2016. Resolving the uncertainty surrounding capital controls would further improve the investment climate, which would temper inflationary pressures and support stronger growth in the medium term. Sustained current account surpluses would create favourable conditions for lifting capital controls. However, the large overhang of króna debt, which may flood out of the country when capital controls are eased, remains a vulnerability (Box 1).

Table 1. **Iceland: Macroeconomic indicators and projections**

Percentage changes, volume (2005 prices)

	2011 Current prices billion ISK	2012	2013	2014	2015	2016
GDP	**1 703.2**	**1.3**	**3.6**	**1.9**	**4.3**	**2.7**
Private consumption	879.0	2.0	0.5	3.7	4.1	2.7
Government consumption	419.4	-1.7	0.7	1.8	2.0	2.5
Gross fixed capital formation	263.7	5.6	-1.0	13.7	17.9	6.7
Final domestic demand	1 562.0	1.6	0.4	4.9	5.9	3.4
Stockbuilding[1]	3.4	0.0	0.0	0.0	-0.3	0.0
Total domestic demand	1 565.4	1.5	0.4	4.7	5.8	3.4
Exports of goods and services	959.9	3.7	6.9	3.1	4.7	4.5
Imports of goods and services	822.1	4.7	0.3	9.9	9.7	6.3
Net exports[1]	137.8	-0.2	3.7	-3.0	-2.0	-0.5
Other items						
Potential GDP		1.4	1.4	1.6	2.0	2.2
Output gap[2]		-4.3	-2.2	-1.9	0.3	0.8
Employment		1.0	3.4	1.6	4.1	1.3
Unemployment rate		6.0	5.4	4.9	3.9	4.1
GDP deflator		3.2	2.0	4.0	6.2	4.0
Consumer price index		5.2	3.9	2.0	2.1	5.1
Core consumer prices		4.6	4.1	2.7	2.6	5.1
Trade balance[3]		6.1	8.2	6.4	7.8	7.7
Current account balance[3]		-4.4	5.8	3.6	2.6	2.8
General government financial balance[3]		-3.7	-2.0	-0.2	0.0	0.1
General government underlying primary balance[3]		2.1	2.4	3.1	3.0	2.9
General government gross debt[4]		95.2	87.7	85.4	81.9	79.3
General government net debt[4]		28.9	27.4	26.1	23.6	22.0
Short-term interest rates		5.5	6.2	6.1	6.0	7.4
Long-term interest rates		6.2	5.8	6.4	6.7	6.5

1. Contributions to changes in real GDP, actual amount in the first column. The sum of contributions can deviate from GDP growth due to chain linking.
2. As a percentage of potential GDP.
3. As a percentage of GDP.
4. As a percentage of GDP. Includes unfunded liabilities of government employee pension plans, which amounted to about 20% of GDP in 2014.

Source: OECD Economic Outlook database (June 2015) updated with incoming information.

Box 1. **Vulnerabilities for the outlook**

There are a number of vulnerabilities for the outlook. The vulnerabilities are low probability events that would create challenges for the economy, but are not included in the baseline.

Vulnerability	Possible outcome
Disorderly exit from capital controls	The process of lifting the capital controls has many possible pitfalls that could prove to be disorderly to the outlook. Failure to reach agreement with creditors may lead to legal challenges if policies are deemed discriminatory. Capital outflows may increase as barriers are progressively relaxed. Domestic financial institutions may also be exposed to shocks during this process, which may result in increased nonperforming loans or strain on liquidity. However, capital adequacy ratios are relatively high in the banking sector.
Wage bargaining complicates macroeconomic policy	Large wage settlements being made during collective bargaining rounds can be destabilising. Substantial pay rises are likely to trigger a significant tightening to bring inflation and inflation expectations under control. High public sector settlements and fiscal measures to secure settlements can undermine the fiscal position.
Rising financial losses of the state-owned Housing Finance Fund (HFF)	The weakness of the Housing Finance Fund could undermine the financial position of the Treasury budget, especially if more losses crystallise quickly. The Housing Finance Fund has already required substantial recapitalisation and the entire stock of HFF debt is guaranteed by the government (Kr. 881 billion, equivalent to 44% of GDP).
Large rises in oil prices	The substantial drop in the price of oil has boosted Iceland's terms-of-trade. A large rebound would undermine some of the improvement in the current account balance.
Euro area weakness	A further intensification of euro area difficulties could further weaken the demand for Icelandic products. A resolution to the current problems and stronger euro area growth represent upside risks for Icelandic exports.
Financial market turbulence	International financial markets may become more volatile and risk premia could jump. These could translate to important shocks for Iceland, undermine some of the progress made in fiscal policy, and affect its external position due to being a net debtor.
Political stalemate	Iceland faces a number of complex challenges, not least with respect to capital controls. Forging political consensus to take the next steps may prove elusive leading to delays in needed reforms.
Natural disaster	Iceland has been periodically affected by volcanic eruptions. Severe eruptions can have damaging impacts on economic activity. However, Iceland has a system of disaster insurance which would mitigate the economic impacts

The outcome of the recent wage bargaining round threatens the recovery. On average, private-sector wages will rise by over 20% between mid-2015 and mid-2018 and even more rapidly for low-income workers. The wage agreements were facilitated by fiscal measures, including tax cuts, at an estimated net cost of 0.5% of GDP. The central bank has raised interest rates in response to these developments and has signalled further increases.

Without deep reform to the collective bargaining system such wage pressures could reoccur (Box 1). While Iceland has many of the same labour market institutions as other Nordic countries (Box 2), these counties have tended to avoid such sharp disputes. Pinpointing the features that support a well-functioning collective bargaining system is difficult (OECD, 2004), but some dimensions may be important and elements of other systems may provide useful examples of alternative approaches for Iceland:

- In Iceland, the wage demands do not appear to take into account macroeconomic externalities. Other systems set reference points for negotiations to limit adverse consequences. For example, in Norway, the sequencing of agreements starts with the internationally-exposed sector, basing the settlement on competitiveness concerns, with that award then influencing subsequent agreements. The natural-resource based

Box 2. **Collective bargaining in Iceland**

The collective bargaining system in Iceland, whilst similar to other Nordic models, has its own peculiarities.

Collective bargaining rounds typically occur every three years with the structure of the pay settlements tending to offer large increases in the first year and smaller increases in subsequent years. Wage demands are often expressed as the cumulative increase over the three years.

The degree of co-ordination amongst the social partners can vary. On the employers' side, the vast majority of firms negotiate under the aegis of the Confederation of Icelandic Employers. On the union side, the right to bargain lies with each union, though this may be transferred to national federations. On occasion, the largest unions form a collective negotiating committee. In the recent bargaining round, on the other hand, the unions did not work together and the employers then negotiated with the larger unions to find a settlement that could serve as a template for other settlements.

The private sector unions' arguments for wage increases can vary, but in the past decade they have tended to concentrate on the lowest wages. The size of the demands tend not to be based on an evaluation of what is consistent with macroeconomic stability, but on wages for other groups. If settlements for some workers have already been made, those awards tend to set a floor for wage demands. In the recent bargaining round, three-year awards of around 25-30% for doctors and teachers led to demands by other unions for 50% pay increases over three years, whereas employers were offering annual increases of 3%.

In the private sector, the centralised contracts typically negotiate a minimum increase for everyone's wages. On top of this increase, sectoral and firm-level negotiations take into account specific local conditions offering top ups. Finally, private firms may grant additional pay rises that contribute to wage drift over the settlement period. In the public sector, negotiations usually follow the private sector, with the award typically based on the minimal wage increase. Top ups to the base are less common in the public sector, partly due to the "flat" nature of public sector occupations, such as teaching, and more recently, to the fiscal consolidation. When relative wages vis-à-vis the private sector get out of line, parity in public sector wages is often restored through industrial action.

When disputes erupt, the social partners can turn to the state mediator. The mediator then leads the negotiations and can submit proposals to the social partners. When these talks break down, industrial action can be initiated if advanced notification is given. The mediator submits a proposal to the social partners if the difference between them is not too large. If the mediator's proposal is rejected, parliament may be required to rule on whether strikes are harmful and thus banned, as was the case in the recent wage bargaining round.

The government has been typically involved in the collective bargaining process. The social partners expect the government to offer tax concessions and social transfers in an effort to encourage moderate settlements. The Government's contribution in the last two negotiation rounds (2011 and 2015) has been unusually large, not least in light of the size of the negotiated wage increases.

export industries in Iceland may provide a poor signal of what the rest of the economy can bear. In Belgium, legislation limits pay awards to forecasts of labour costs in neighbouring countries. The Icelandic government has proposed the establishment of a macroeconomic council to provide information on the state of the economy before the collective bargaining round, which goes some way in this direction.

- With many different agreements needing to be reached (around 400 in Iceland), the potential for co-ordination failures can arise with different agreements trying to get their members the largest award. The degree of co-ordination in other Nordic systems appears to be relatively high, which helps reduce this type of problem.
- Public sector wage growth tends to lag behind the private sector and relative wage levels are reset during the wage bargaining rounds. This leads to periodic large wage adjustments. Such catch-up awards helped trigger the large wage demands in the recent collective bargaining round. In other countries, such as Denmark, partial indexation of public sector wages to the private sector limits how far relative wages get out of line.
- When impasse is reached a state mediator can intervene in both Iceland and other Nordic countries. However, in other countries the powers of the mediator appear stronger. In Denmark, the state mediator can propose an agreement - generally costly to both sides - that can be made into law if ultimately necessary. In other cases, such as Luxembourg, the wage bargaining system requires considerable negotiation and the use of mediation and arbitration before industrial action can commence. Iceland's state mediator could be given greater authority to arbitrate in favour of realistic wage settlements, in line with practices in these countries.

Lifting capital controls while preserving financial stability

Iceland imposed capital controls in the wake of the banking collapse in 2008. Although lifting these controls is desirable for long-term prospects, doing so risks disorderly capital outflows in the short run. These outflows would include foreign claims on domestic assets locked in the insolvent estates of the failed banks (which could unleash capital amounting to between 25% and 45% of GDP), carry trade funds trapped in Iceland (sometimes called offshore króna holdings, which now amount to around 15% of GDP), and the potential for an abrupt rebalancing of pension funds and other domestic investment portfolios toward foreign assets (which could amount to roughly 35% of GDP).

In consultation with the IMF, the central bank initially issued a two-step plan in 2011 that aimed gradually to:

- channel unstable offshore króna holdings to longer-term investors until the stock was manageable relative to official reserve holdings, and then
- ease the controls, possibly using exit taxes or incentives to slow outflows and redirect funds toward domestic assets.

The central bank implemented the first part of the plan by holding foreign exchange auctions that have gradually trimmed offshore króna holdings from about 40% of GDP in 2008 to 15% of GDP in late 2014. Despite this success, the plan had a shortcoming because it failed to address the threat from the insolvent bank estates, which only later became apparent. The realisation of this threat compelled the authorities to broaden the capital controls to cover the estates in 2012, and rendered the previous plan insufficient.

Despite the absence of a concrete plan, significant steps have been taken to pave the way for liberalising controls. Steps have been taken to fortify the financial system, including regular meetings of a newly created Financial Stability Council since the fall of 2014 and the Central Bank's introduction of rules on bank foreign currency funding ratios and liquidity.

In June 2015, the authorities announced a plan to unwind both the failed banks' estates and the remaining offshore króna. The plan was formed in consultation with a task force of outside experts (including economists and legal experts on international taxation) appointed by the government in July 2014. The plan to resolve the insolvent estates uses a combination of incentives to motivate the boards charged with winding up the failed banks to reach voluntary agreements with their claim holders to allocate remaining assets in a way that does not compromise financial stability. Specifically, the authorities will only accept composition plans that satisfy specified stability conditions, including:

- measures to neutralise the threat from distributing króna-denominated assets, such as making an offsetting "stability contribution" to the Icelandic treasury;
- extending the maturity of foreign-currency denominated domestic assets (such as foreign exchange bank deposits) to terms of 7 to 10 years; and
- refinancing or otherwise ensuring the repayment of foreign-exchange denominated loans granted by the authorities to the new banks following the crisis.

Estates that fail to reach a suitable composition agreement by end of 2015 will be subject to a one-time "stability tax" on their total assets holdings of 39% – roughly in the line with the total proportion of all domestic assets in all three estates (Króna denominated or otherwise). Estates can reduce their tax liability to some extent by converting liquid foreign-currency holdings to longer-term assets. To unwind the offshore króna, the authorities plan to employ a one-time auction that will allow foreign investors to either convert short-term króna assets into Icelandic government bonds or to foreign exchange at a cost. Unconverted funds will be locked in non-interest bearing accounts, thereby discouraging holdouts.

Although this plan is subject to litigation risks, the winding-up boards of the three estates, in consultation with their largest stakeholders, have proposed composition agreements to the authorities that satisfy the stability conditions. Each proposal would require approval from estate stakeholders representing at least 70% of the claimants and 60% of the total value of claims. The government estimates that the stability tax would generate a one-time boost in treasury revenues ranging between about 34% and 42% of 2014 GDP, compared to revenues between 18% and 32% of 2014 GDP for composition agreements.

The authorities recently announced measures that begin to address the threat of capital outflows from private portfolio rebalancing. Pension funds will be allowed to apply to the central bank for exemptions to purchase foreign assets over the remainder of 2015 amounting to as much as ½ percent of GDP overall, allocated amongst applicants based upon a weighting of their size and net inflows. To facilitate further portfolio rebalancing, it would be sensible to continue to place temporary restrictions on private foreign asset purchases that can be adjusted in light of balance payments conditions.

The Icelandic authorities are also working with the OECD's Investment Committee and its Advisory Task Force on the Codes of Liberalisation of Capital Movements and Current Invisible Operations. When Iceland imposed capital controls it received a derogation from the obligations of the Codes under Article 7.

Low inflation is threatened by high wage settlements

Monetary policy has successfully reduced inflation, and low inflation has allowed the central bank to reduce its policy rates from their peak after the crisis. Combined with capital controls, this contributed to exchange rate stability. Amendments to central bank legislation in 2001 and 2009 created a framework that has contributed to these successes, including setting up a monetary policy committee with a clear mandate for monetary policy and measures to promote accountability. The government is currently considering changes to the Central Bank Act. Any changes should not undermine the actual or perceived independence of monetary policy, especially in the light of political pressures on the central bank that have undermined its credibility in the past. For example, ensuring that appointments to the monetary policy committee continue to be made on the basis of expertise rather than political orientation would help safeguard perceived independence.

Monetary policy is particularly challenging in Iceland, given the tiny size of the economy and challenges posed by international capital mobility. Iceland's withdrawal from consideration for EU accession has for the moment removed the option of joining the euro area, a possibility raised in the previous *Economic Survey*. Past attempts at pegging the króna have been unsuccessful, suggesting that foreign exchange interventions can at most only smooth erratic and transitory fluctuations.

Once capital controls are lifted, monetary policy should focus on inflation stability in the medium term and allow the exchange rate to float. To this extent, bolstering credibility and reputation can help anchor expectations and reduce the degree of exchange-rate pass-through, hence limiting output losses linked to fighting inflation.

Monetary policy is poorly equipped to offset the effects of supply shocks, which are especially destabilising in Iceland given its small size and limited production base. As such, monetary policy needs to be complemented by enhanced flexibility in the economy and by the maintenance of fiscal and financial buffers that help mitigate effects from economic and financial shocks.

The implementation of monetary policy could be made easier if the inflation targeting framework were refined to reflect national circumstances. In particular, policy implementation is particularly challenging because of high exchange-rate pass through; exchange rate movements can cause pronounced short-term swings in inflation that largely play out within two years. Attempts to smooth through pass-through effects likely compound instability due to policy lags, the bluntness of monetary policy instruments, and any tendency to react asymmetrically to inflationary and disinflationary shocks. Hence, it may be desirable to lengthen the horizon for achieving the inflation target and craft policy communication to focus attention away from transitory inflationary disturbances. Such measures would help to anchor longer-term inflationary expectations and thereby enhance credibility.

Bolstering macro-prudential policy and prudential regulation

To deal with systemic threats, a Financial Stability Council has been created. It brings together the Ministry of Finance, the Governor of the Central Bank and the Director General of the Financial Supervision Authority and is supported by a systemic risk committee. Macro-prudential policy to ensure financial stability will be based on a number of operational concerns, such as credit growth and leverage, but will also examine ways to reduce moral hazard and address the effects of excessive capital flows. One important consideration will be embedding actions to address excessive capital flows in Iceland's international obligations on capital flows, including the OECD Codes of Liberalisation of Capital Movements. An agreed set of capital flow management instruments as part of the macroprudential policy framework would reduce the vulnerability of the economy to abrupt swings in capital flows unrelated to fundamentals. Finally, the central bank could further enhance credibility by maintaining large foreign exchange reserves as an additional safeguard.

Actions to tighten prudential regulation have already been substantial and go a long way to building up buffers in the financial sector. The main initiatives in bank regulation has been to phase in, between the end of 2014 and 2017, increases in the liquidity coverage ratio, particularly for foreign currency, and raising funding rules to reduce the risks of term and currency mismatches. With its membership of the European Economic Area, Iceland is committed to adopting European Union financial regulation, which concerns capital requirements, bank resolution and deposit insurance, areas where reforms were recommended in the 2013 *Economic Survey*. As a result, considerable progress has been made in building up buffers in the financial sector, particularly the banks. The Icelandic authorities are already at - or close to - the international frontier in prudential regulation through the timely implementation of Basel III. Remaining at the frontier by keeping up with international norms and using stress tests to evaluate the robustness of the financial sector will help maintain the health of the financial sector.

Recommendations for lifting capital controls while preserving financial stability

- Progress is needed in lifting Iceland's capital controls and the current plan is a welcome step in this direction. Maintaining a robust macroeconomic stability framework will help avoid a disorderly outcome.
- Monetary policy needs to raise interest rates to ensure that a wage-price spiral does not develop, as already stated by the Monetary Policy Committee. The focus should remain on low and stable inflation over the medium term, while allowing the exchange rate to float apart from limited interventions to smooth erratic fluctuations.
- To protect macroeconomic stability the central bank should remain independent from political interference. The monetary policy committee introduced in 2009 should be retained.
- Strengthen the macro-prudential policy framework, incorporating tools to address large swings in capital flows unrelated to fundamentals, while respecting international commitments.
- To protect the economy from unavoidable shocks and reinforce confidence, buffers should be built up including ample fiscal space, foreign exchange reserves and bank capital and liquidity.
- Reforms to current labour market institutions are needed, including giving the state mediator more resources and power to arbitrate in favour of realistic wage agreements.

Additional recommendations

- To safeguard the perceived independence of monetary policy appointments to the committee should be for staggered fixed terms and should continue to be made on the basis of professional experience.

Securing long-term fiscal sustainability

Fiscal policy has succeeded in eliminating the budget deficit and lowering public debt (Figure 5). Public debt has started to decline, which, combined with a little change in financial assets, brought down net government financial liabilities by around 2% of GDP in 2014. While some of the progress has been helped by one offs (such as dividends from the banks; also the planned partial privatisation of the state-owned bank Landsbankinn

Figure 5. **Public finances have improved**

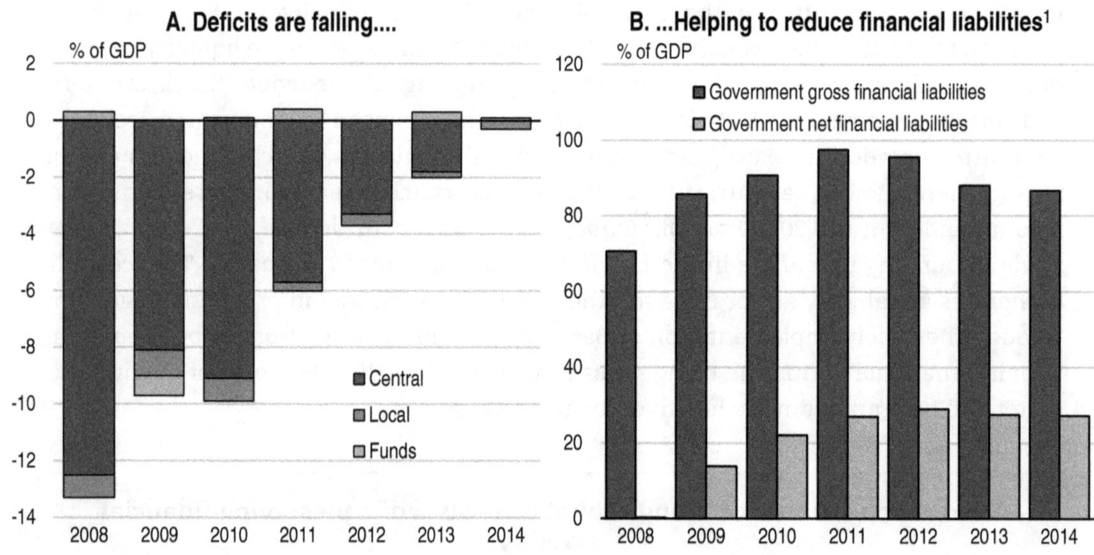

1. The figures on Panel B exclude unfunded public pensions liabilities.
Source: OECD, Analytical database and Statistics Iceland.

StatLink http://dx.doi.org/10.1787/888933258453

should be used to reduce debt), the underlying improvement in the primary balance is sufficient to put gross debt on a downward trajectory.

Iceland's fiscal policy is currently on track to achieve sustainability and lower debt, but relaxing fiscal policy risks derailing this process and reverting to unsustainable trends. Projections can shed light on the consequences of different deficits and use of windfall resources on debt sustainability (Figure 6). The projections are based on macroeconomic assumptions for growth and interest rates, and evaluate the path of gross debt (the government uses a slightly different debt measure, but the implications hold for either measure). Keeping the budget balanced in line with current plans would reduce gross debt to about 60% of GDP in 2040 (assuming that government financial assets remain constant relative to GDP at the level of 2013) and virtually eliminate the net debt position (when not considering contingent liabilities and unfunded public pension schemes). If the proceeds from the sale of Landsbankinn and the stability contributions are used to retire debt, gross debt declines more rapidly and would drop below 40% of GDP by the end of the projections. However, the apparent favourableness of the current fiscal position should not give grounds for complacency as relaxing fiscal discipline could easily undermine sustainability. If fiscal policy reverts to past performance by running a 2% deficit on average, and the one-off and windfall revenues are not used to pay down debt, gross debt begins to mount again and approaches 100% of GDP in 2040.

Sizeable pressures on fiscal policy remain

With risks that fiscal policy could be thrown off track, policymakers need to remain focused on debt reduction. Reducing gross debt would lower very high borrowing costs (effective interest rate of about 5½ per cent) that exceed the return on government financial assets (about 2%). Another reason to reduce financial liabilities is the shortfall in funding for state pensions (the implicit debt is currently estimated to be around 20-25% of

Figure 6. **Simulations of public debt paths**

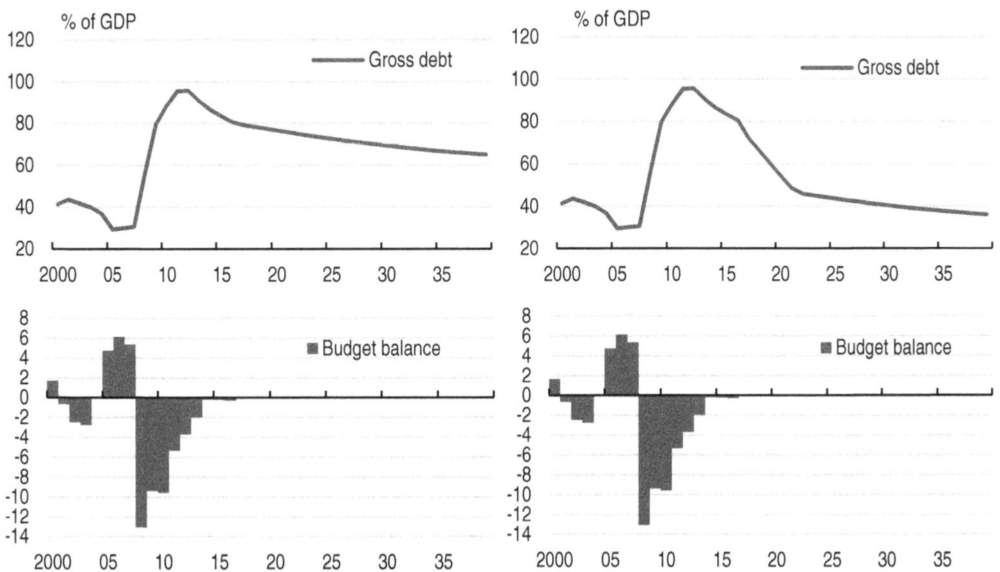

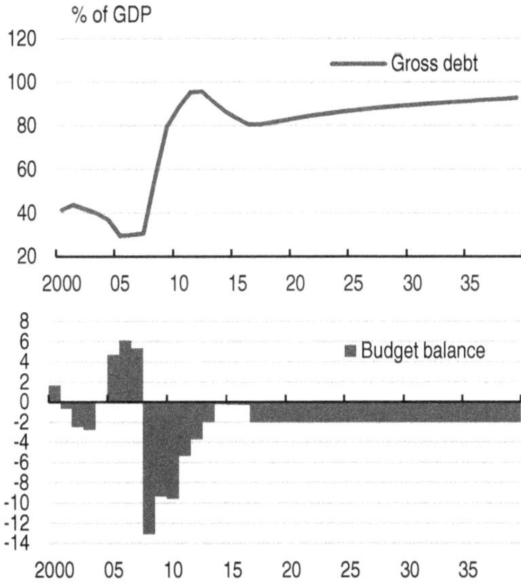

Note: Simulations follow the OECD projection through 2016. Thereafter, real GDP growth averages 2.4% and inflation averages 2.5%. In simulations shown in panels A and C, financial assets are kept constant at their latest projected level (57.3%).

Source: OECD, Economic Outlook database and OECD calculations.

StatLink http://dx.doi.org/10.1787/888933258468

GDP). Finally, creating larger fiscal buffers would allow the government to react to future destabilising economic or financial shocks, including a disorderly lifting of capital controls.

The government has financial assets of around 60% of GDP, but not all of them can be counted on if government finances were to come under short-term pressure. At the end of

2013, government financial assets included currency and deposits worth 22% of GDP, shares and other equity worth 21% of GDP, as well as loans and other accounts receivable amounting to 16% of GDP. Around 25% of GDP of government assets are foreign exchange reserves for use by the central bank. Other financial assets may be hard to draw upon in an emergency. For example government holdings of Landsbankinn require parliament's approval to sell additional shares and, in a crisis, fire-sale prices may prevail.

Large contingent liabilities in the form of state guarantees suggest that the measured net debt position may be somewhat flattering. A large financial risk is the Housing Finance Fund (HFF), which has facilitated access to mortgage loans with a state guarantee. The HFF has struggled recently as commercial banks offer lower interest rates, drawing away new mortgage growth, while existing customers have prepaid in large numbers. Coupled with a default rate of around 8%, the HFF has made losses, requiring the state to recapitalise it periodically (around 50 billion króna so far, 2.5% of 2014 GDP). The total state guarantee to the HFF is worth around 881 billion króna (44% of 2014 GDP). The current plan of winding down the HFF is therefore appropriate. Instead of using the HFF to provide universal support to homeownership, Iceland should target its financial aid to low-income families who wish to rent – a more effective and less expensive approach.

A second large source of contingent liabilities arises from world aluminium prices. State guarantees are in place for the largest energy company, Landsvirkjun. As around one-half of electricity sales are linked to the aluminium price, the company (and indirectly the government) is therefore exposed to commodity price risks. The state guarantee to Landsvirkjun is estimated at around 300 billion króna or 15% of GDP in 2014. No further state guarantee to such industrial development should be undertaken as has been the case more recently with Landsvirkjun.

Adopting a new fiscal framework

The government has prepared a fiscal framework for long-term sustainability and to secure space for counter-cyclical stabilisation. The fiscal rules built into the proposed Organic Budget law limit the deficit to 2.5% of GDP in any given year and require the cumulative balance over a 5 year period to be positive. They also target public debt of 30% of GDP (public debt is defined as gross financial liabilities less unfunded pension liabilities and other accounts payable, as well as the value of currency and deposit assets; in 2014 debt by this measure was about 55% of GDP). When debt is above the target, the government must reduce it by 1/20 of the difference annually. While this should see government debt brought down, any slippage could see debt loads rising again.

The budget law would also hold the government accountable for its fiscal policy, including through the creation of an independent fiscal council. Newly-elected governments must present a statement of objectives for fiscal policy and the annual budget must be linked to medium-term fiscal policy objectives. Anchoring the annual budget on medium-term objectives should mitigate the risk of relaxing spending control towards the top of the cycle. The law also aims to make fiscal policy more predictable and less susceptible to the tendency for adjustments to be introduced during the budget year. Assessing progress of fiscal policy against the fiscal rules and evaluating longer-term sustainability are areas where the fiscal council could develop its role.

Better targeting fiscal policy

The 2015 budget introduces several initiatives to support growth and inclusiveness: higher spending on health and education; further investment on transportation infrastructure; more generous child benefits; and a switch towards indirect taxation. On the eve of the reform, the VAT revenue ratio, which gives an indication of the efficiency relative to a benchmark of uniform rates and full VAT compliance, was below that of many other countries (Figure 7). The reform should improve overall efficiency by raising the reduced rate (from 7 to 11%), while reducing the standard rate, which was amongst the highest in the OECD (from 25.5 to 24%). The reform also abolishes a commodity tax levied on consumption goods. The distributional impact of the tax reform will be modest. A further reduction in VAT exemptions and narrowing the gap between the reduced and standard rates would make the system more neutral and easier to administer. Greater VAT revenue could facilitate a reduced reliance on direct taxes, which account for a significantly higher share of revenue than the OECD average (45% and 34%, respectively).

Figure 7. **VAT performance could be improved**

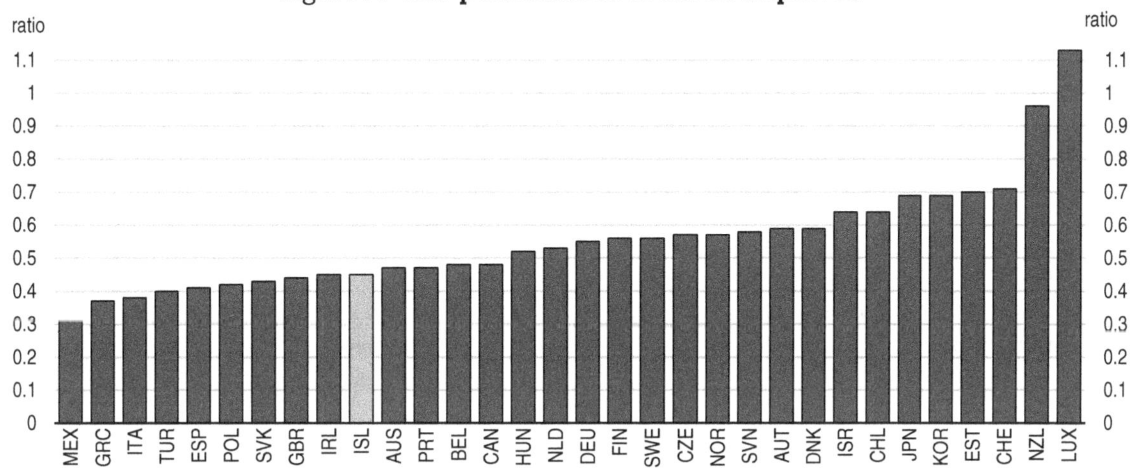

Note: The VAT revenue ratio (VRR) measures the ratio of the VAT revenue actually collected to what would theoretically be raised if VAT was applied at the standard rate to the entire potential tax base in a "pure" VAT regime and all revenue was collected.
Source: OECD, Consumption Tax Trends (2014).

StatLink http://dx.doi.org/10.1787/888933258475

Disability is rising

Disability benefits account for a large and rising share of public social spending. Life expectancy is high in Iceland (particularly for women) and the share of people who report that they are in good or very good health is substantially higher than the average for the OECD (OECD, 2013c). However, enrolment in disability programmes has been rising (Figure 8). Disability and sickness programmes are amongst the most costly in the OECD, accounting for over one fifth of all social spending (OECD, 2010). A large proportion of those receiving benefits are women and persons with low education outcomes.

Young people can be reliant on benefits

Since 2007, the percentage of young people not in employment, education or training (NEET) has risen more than on average for the OECD (Carcillo *et al*, 2015). This increase reflects the impact of the crisis on the young, which has seen their unemployment rate rise to over 10% in 2013, and growing disability rolls, which accounted for around 3% of those aged between 20

Figure 8. **Disability rolls are rising**

Percentage of the population receiving a disability pension or allowance.

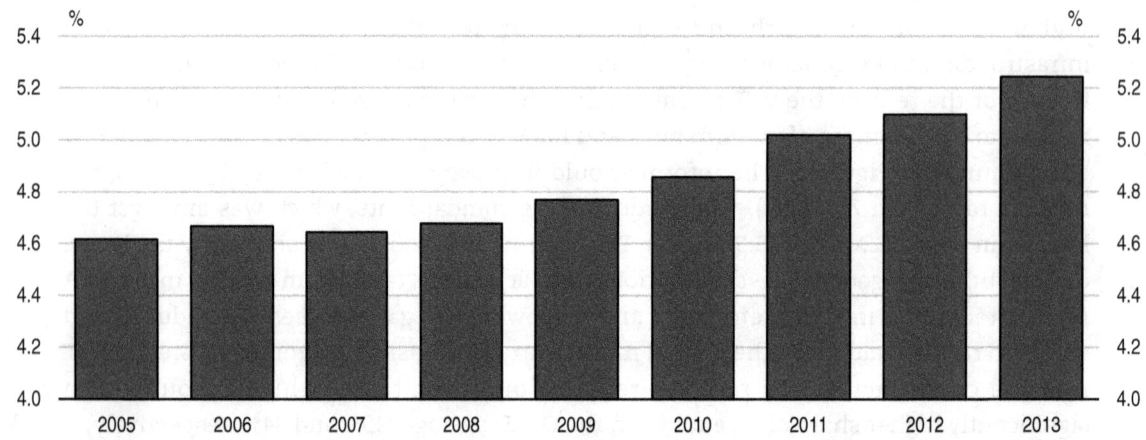

Source: Tryggingastofnun.

StatLink http://dx.doi.org/10.1787/888933258485

and 25. Survey evidence indicates that over 13% of the youth in Iceland received either unemployment or disability benefits at some point during 2012, while the OECD average was around 9% (Carcillo *et al.*, 2015). The large number receiving unemployment benefits is partly an outcome of a high labour force participation rate amongst the young (almost 79% in Iceland for those aged between 15 and 24 compared to the OECD average of just over 47% in 2013). Iceland is unusual in having the longest duration of unemployment benefits (recently reduced from 36 to 30 months) with the shortest contribution period for eligibility (3 months). The young can also qualify for disability benefits and means tested benefits (including when living with their parents). This system reduces poverty. However, reducing the incentives to drop out of the labour force provided by current support mechanisms and working to reintegrate those with weak labour market attachment would also reduce poverty and absorb fewer fiscal resources. Helping people back to work and avoiding scarring (which amongst the young can be damaging for career prospects) may require training and retraining, which underlines the importance of improving outcomes in education.

Recommendations for fiscal policy sustainability

- Pass and implement the Organic Budget Law, including enacting the balanced budget rules and establishing an independent Fiscal Council to assess progress towards sustainability.
- Use windfall gains and one-off revenues to pay down debt, including any proceeds from lifting the capital controls.
- Avoid accumulating further contingent liabilities, including by closing the Housing Financing Fund (HFF).
- Further shift tax revenue from income taxes to VAT, while preserving equity.

Additional recommendations

- To preserve labour force attachment and reduce fiscal costs, help people get back to work, tighten access to welfare benefits and further reduce the duration of unemployment benefits.

Supporting long-term productivity growth

Despite economic recovery, Iceland's GNI per capita remains below the average of other Nordic economies and near the OECD average (Figure 9). This largely reflects weak labour productivity, which slumped after the crisis, although multifactor productivity has held up (Figure 11). Compared with other Nordic countries, productivity shortfalls are apparent across all sectors apart from fishing and energy-intensive metallurgy (particularly aluminium). With labour force participation already high, stronger growth will require more business investment and higher multifactor productivity growth (Figure 11. Panel D). Addressing the relative mediocrity of income would help boost an aspect of well-being where Iceland performs quite poorly (Box 6).

Iceland's business sector has four main components (McKinsey, 2012). The capital intensive resource-based sector - fisheries and metallurgy – combined with tourism account for the majority of exports. A smaller international sector consists of other firms exposed to international competition, including business and ICT services, as well as some manufacturing. The remaining two sectors are the public sector and private domestic services, which together account for 70% of employment. Outside the metallurgy sector, foreign ownership is low, partly as a result of restrictions but also due to the strong presence of state-ownership in the energy sector.

Figure 9. **GNI per capita is slightly above average**

2013 estimates in US dollars, current prices, current PPPs

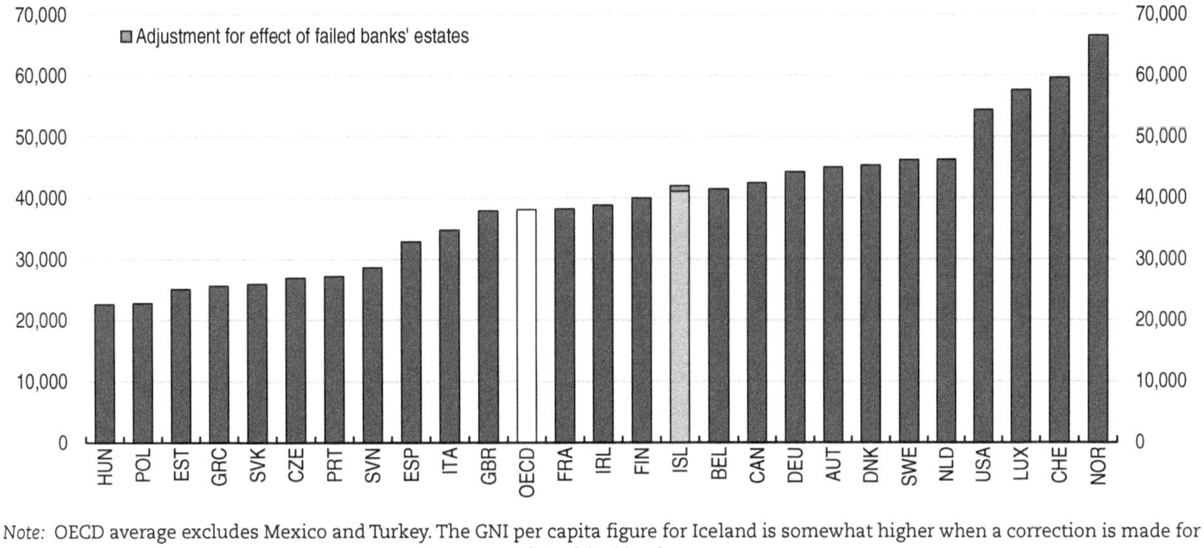

Note: OECD average excludes Mexico and Turkey. The GNI per capita figure for Iceland is somewhat higher when a correction is made for estimates of service payments sent abroad by the estates of the failed banks.

Source: OECD, National Accounts database, Central Bank of Iceland (adjustments)

StatLink http://dx.doi.org/10.1787/888933258490

Recent developments are somewhat disquieting from the perspective of the longer term. Booms in specific sectors, such as fishing, energy, aluminium and finance, all contributed to rapid expansions but were also followed by slowdowns or crashes. Unfortunately, positive spillovers from these sectors to other sectors have been limited due to sector-specificity of skills or a high degree of capital intensity. Furthermore, the deals made to attract energy-intensive investments, with large multinationals that can credibly threaten to invest elsewhere, have led to Iceland capturing a relatively small share of the

Box 3. **Well-being in Iceland**

Well-being in Iceland is high in comparison with the rest of the OECD. According to the OECD's Better Life Index, residents enjoy high levels of employment, community engagement, environmental services, health and life satisfaction. On the other hand, Iceland's rankings for housing, civic engagement, work-life balance and particularly income and wealth are only average at best (Figure 10). Per capita income in comparison with the rest of the OECD has dropped over time and was hit by the crisis.

Figure 10. **Well-being is high in Iceland**

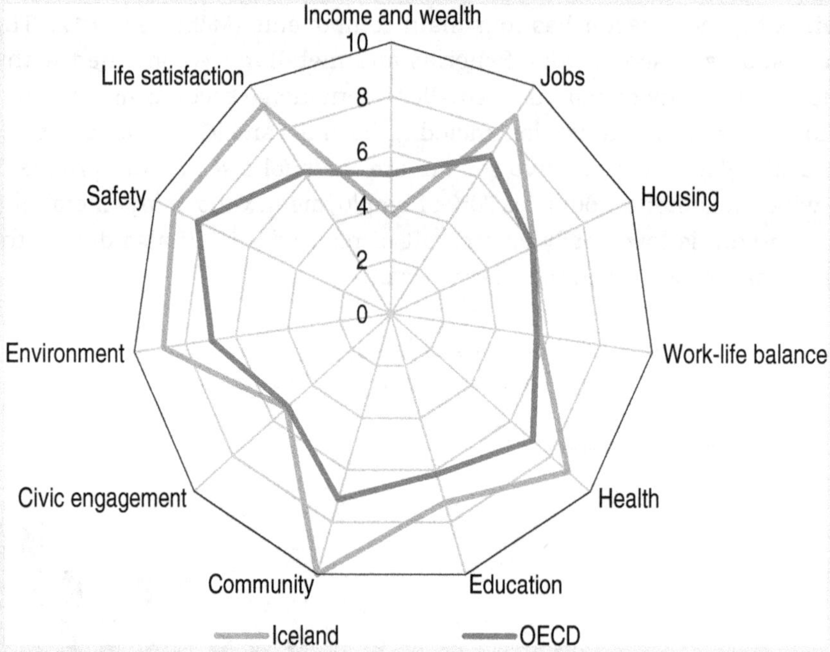

Note: Each well-being dimension is measured by one to three indicators from the OECD Better Life indicator set. Normalized indicators are averaged with equal weights. Indicators are normalized to range between 10 (best) and 0 according to the following formula: (indicator value - minimum value) / (maximum value - minimum value).

Source: OECD, Better Life Index indicators 2014.

StatLink http://dx.doi.org/10.1787/888933258502

resource rent. A proposal to capture more of the resource rent by laying an electricity transmission cable to Scotland has not been fully fleshed out and how the resource rent would be shared is unresolved.

The current boom is based to some extent on the rapid development of the tourism sector. With one million visitors in 2014, this is welcome, but it tends to create relatively low-skilled low-wage jobs and comes with limited opportunities for productivity growth. Against the draw of migrants to the booming low-skill jobs, the Icelandic economy is experiencing outmigration of high-skilled people. Furthermore, unemployment amongst university graduates is rising, suggesting mismatch. As such, and despite the economic recovery, Iceland remains in transition away from a largely resource-dependent development model, but a new growth model that also draws on the strong human capital stock in Iceland has yet to emerge.

Figure 11. **Productivity developments in Iceland**

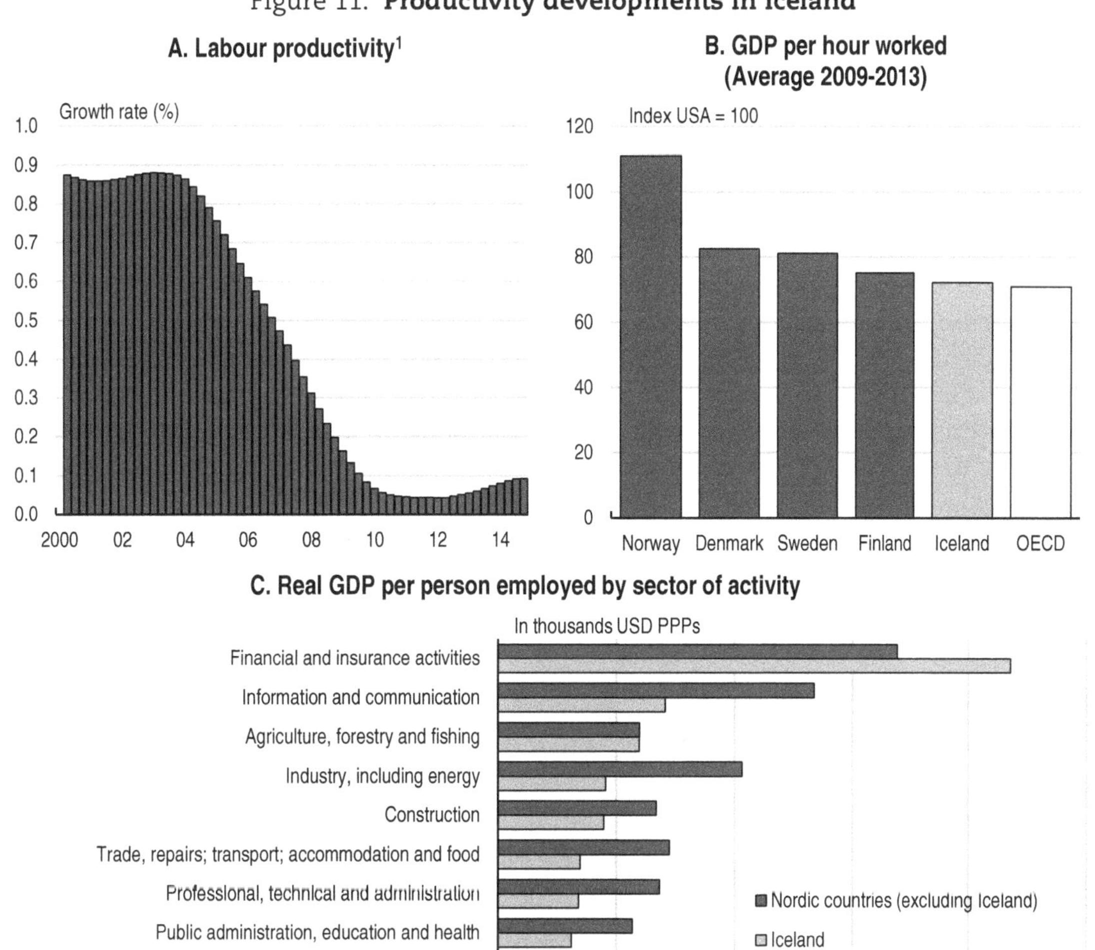

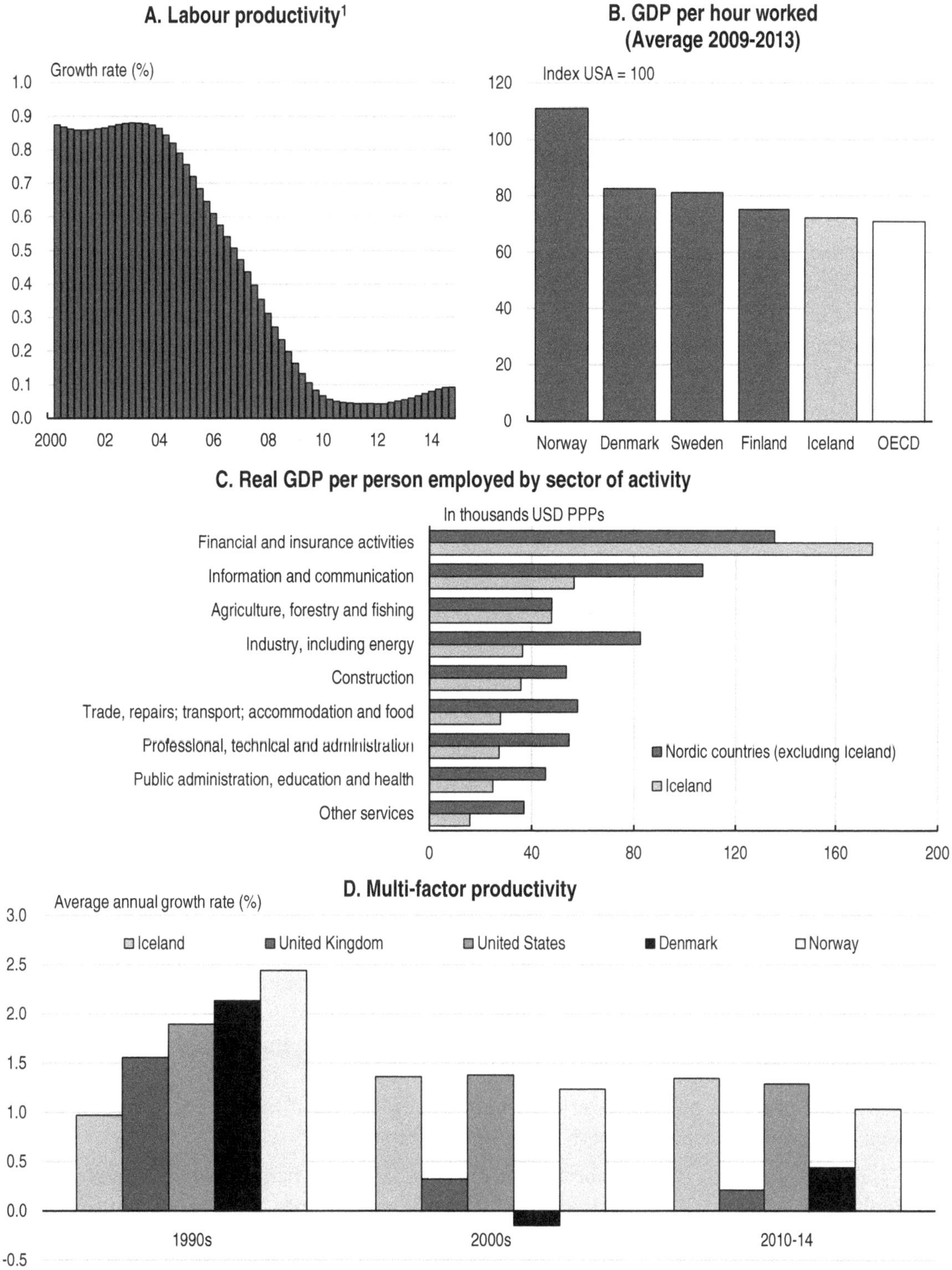

1. Time series smoothed using a Hodrick-Prescott filter.

Source: OECD, Analytical and Economic Outlook databases; Labour Force Statistics and Productivity databases.

StatLink http://dx.doi.org/10.1787/888933258510

Against this backdrop, there have been calls for reorienting Iceland's growth strategy towards more balanced development. A forum was established in 2013 to discuss a growth strategy, with the members including political and business leaders as well as academics and representatives of the labour unions. However, progress thus far has been modest. In this context, supporting the work of the growth forum with a dedicated body, such as a productivity or growth commission, would help identify and prioritise the policies which are the most conducive to improving the business environment overall. Such a body would play an important role in undertaking or commissioning the necessary research and analysis to identify the most promising growth-enhancing policies for Iceland. The productivity commission would also help move the debate forward by championing productivity-enhancing reforms and thereby help overcome resistance from particular interest groups. Furthermore, the advocacy role would help build constituencies supporting these reforms, particularly where entrenched interests may be resistant, raising the likelihood of better policies being introduced. Improving product market regulation will play an important role in this agenda.

Improving product market regulation

Iceland's regulatory framework for product markets is close to the OECD average when measured by the OECD's overall product market regulation indicator (Figure 12). This is in line with indicators for Norway and Sweden, but more restrictive than the case for Denmark and Finland. But performance in Iceland is poorer for regulations creating barriers to entrepreneurship, with the complexity of regulatory procedures noticeably more restrictive.

The number of newly registered firms in Iceland has dropped significantly from the peaks just before the financial crisis, although those rates were likely unsustainable (Figure 13). Reducing barriers to entrepreneurship is important for both boosting employment and productivity. Recent empirical evidence suggests that new firms contribute importantly to employment growth (Criscuolo *et al.*, 2014) and that a growing share of start-ups in a sector is associated with higher productivity growth (Adelet McGowan et al, 2015).

While there are few administrative barriers to establishing a company and progress has been made recently to facilitate doing so online, other barriers to entry are somewhat more pronounced in Iceland. The complexity of regulatory procedures in the licensing and permitting systems and regulatory protection of incumbent (particularly due to legal barriers) are high in comparison with other OECD countries. In this light, the government should review the number of licences and permits required and simplify regulations. Additional progress should be made in reviewing the legal barriers to entry in the electricity, air transport and airport, and seaport sectors.

The government has supported the creation of small firms through innovation incubators, which are often clustered by sector to promote knowledge spillovers. Experience so far has been positive with the existing eight incubators attracting a lot of promising entrepreneurs and links with universities being established. As this is still a relatively new initiative, the government should evaluate the effectiveness of these programmes with the aim to adjust them as needed to achieve the maximum impact.

For Iceland, one of the important constraints on entrepreneurship is the lack of venture capital. Partly, the lack of funds reflects the uncertainty surrounding capital

Figure 12. **Barriers to entrepreneurship is relatively restrictive in areas**

Indicator scale of 0-6 from least to most restrictive

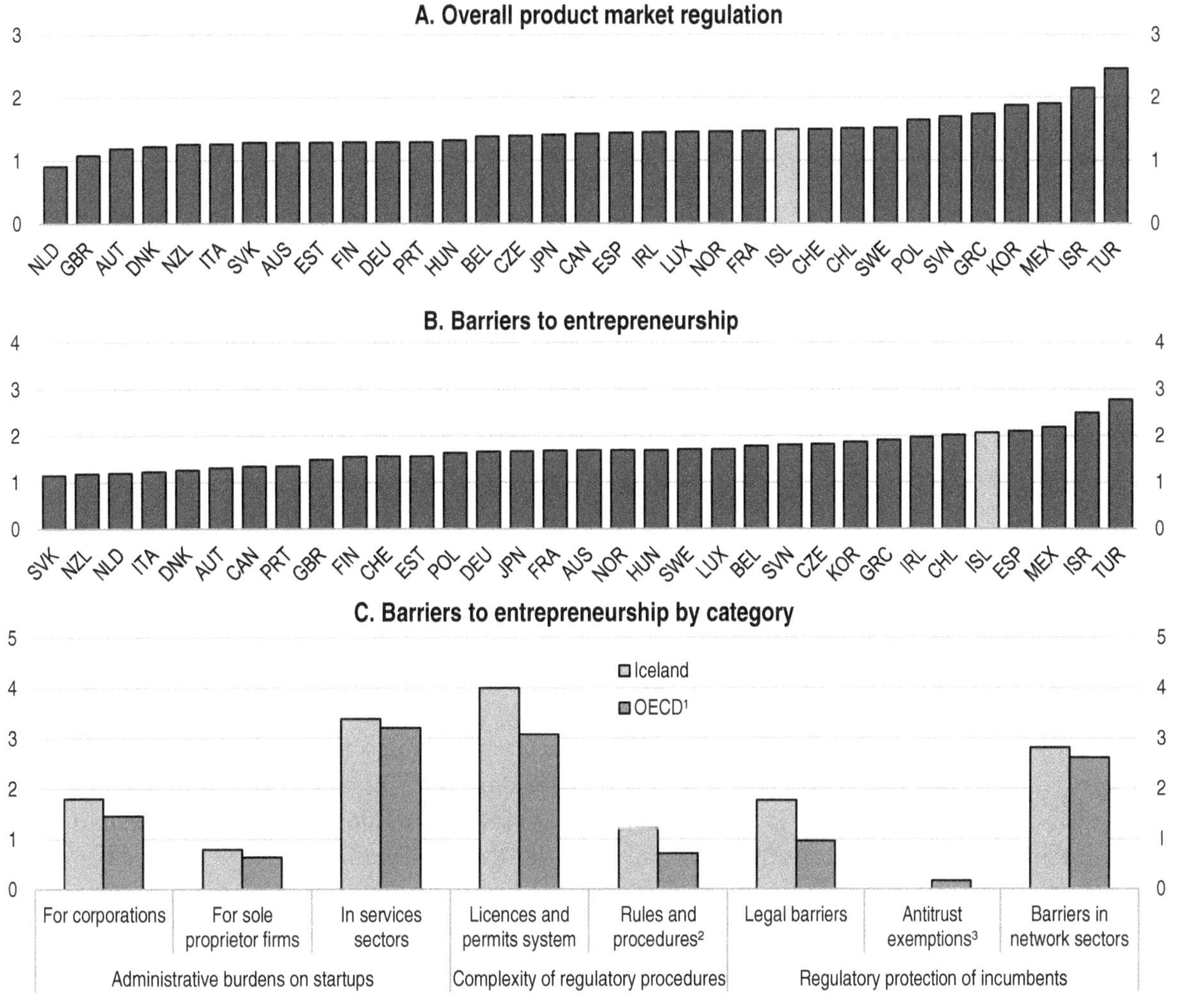

1. The OECD aggregate is an average of data available (25-30 countries depending on the year covered).
2. Communication and simplification of rules and procedures.
3. Zero for Iceland.

Source: OECD (2013), Product Market Regulation Database, www.oecd.org/economy/pmr.

StatLink http://dx.doi.org/10.1787/888933258523

controls, which will dissipate when they are relaxed. High risk premia associated with macroeconomic volatility also play a role, reinforcing the need for strong macroeconomic policy. Pooling risks in a country as small as Iceland is difficult. One way around this is to have the government pool risks, and it has stepped into this arena by establishing funds, one with the involvement of domestic financial institutions, to promote start-ups that can compete internationally. However, overall funding remains modest.

Another approach to pooling is to involve foreign investors. According to the OECD FDI Restrictiveness Index, however, Iceland has one of the most restrictive regimes for foreign investors. In particular, entry is severely constrained in fishing, electricity and to a lesser extent some parts of transportation, often through limitations on equity participation. The government is working on simplifying the legal framework for investment by non-residents in business enterprises.

Figure 13. **Firm creation has slowly recovered and bankruptcies increased**

New registrations of limited liability companies and number of bankruptcies

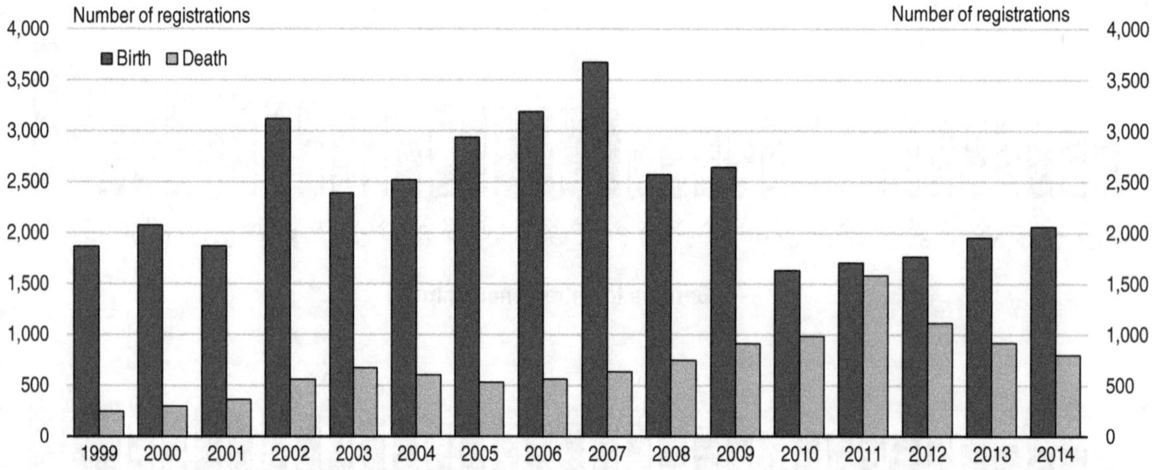

Source: Statistics Iceland

StatLink http://dx.doi.org/10.1787/888933258539

Harnessing competitive pressures

Achieving effective competition can also be a challenge in a small economy when even modest economies to scale imply that the market can support only a single or just a few firms. Indeed, in a number of markets (financial, transport, telecoms, food) only a handful of companies exist or a single firm occupies a dominant position. Where a natural monopoly element is important in a market, separating the competitive segment and setting access rules for the monopoly element can encourage competition. The competition authority repeatedly clashed with the incumbent telecom operator until 2012, when both sides reached agreement to restructure the group into separate companies for retail and wholesale operations, thereby allowing more competition to emerge in the retail segment.

Despite the constraints imposed by the small size of the economy, over the past decade the Icelandic Competition Authority has concluded more than 17 major enforcement cases on abuse of dominant position and 14 major cases on cartels or tacit collusion. Smaller cases are not concluded. In this context, applying the OECD's "Competition Assessment Toolkit" may be particularly helpful. The toolkit provides a means to identify pro-competitive reforms, including removing unnecessary restraints and proposing alternative less restrictive policies to achieve government objectives.

Another potential factor could undermine effective competition. After the crisis, the high indebtedness of many domestic firms made the banks important stakeholders in firms' decisions. This degree of concentration and possible conflict of interest requires careful monitoring. The slow process of restructuring, which is reflected in the delayed rise in bankruptcy following the crisis (Figure 13), created uncertainty about firm ownership. The competition authorities have acted by setting limits on when the company had to be sold and imposing conditions to ensure fair competition between companies owned by banks and other companies (such as requiring a normal rate of return and preserving the independence of the firm).

In some cases, the authorities may need to be more aggressive in pursuing competitive outcomes. For example, complaints that the low-cost carrier Wow Air could not obtain slots at Keflavik airport to allow it to take advantage of international transfers (and thus compete with Icelandair) have not been resolved despite the efforts of the competition authority and the fact that the slot allocation mechanism was recognised as detrimental to competition as early as 2008 (*OECD* Competition Committee, 2014).

The OECD's Services Trade Restrictiveness Index shows that in a number of sectors restrictions are more binding that the average in the OECD (Figure 14). Restrictions on foreign entry and movements on people were the most important factors, which are related to the barriers to entrepreneurship noted in domestic product market regulation. In part the restrictions were higher due to the imposition of capital controls. Competition could therefore be sharpened through trade more generally. The introduction during 2014 of a bilateral trade agreement with China is a step in this direction. The recent step back from European Union accession need not reduce competitive pressures because the European Economic Area agreement opens borders, even if it does not cover all sectors of the economy.

Figure 14. **Iceland's service trade restrictiveness index across sectors**

The indices take values between zero and one (the most restrictive)[1]

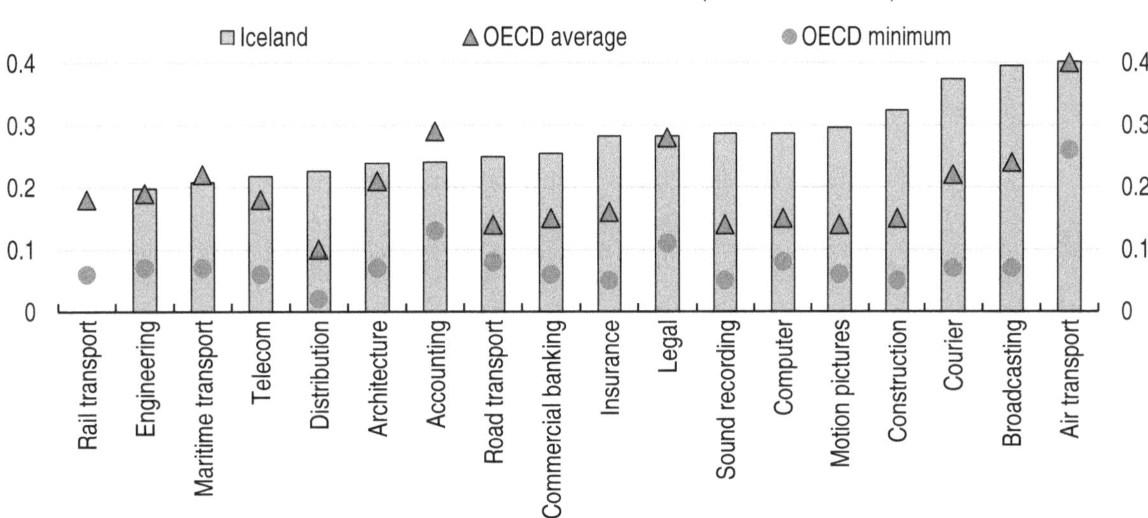

1.The index includes regulatory transparency, barriers to competition, other discriminatory measures, restrictions on movement of people and restrictions on foreign entry. The STRI methodology takes into account different market and trade cost structures across sectors to ensure that they reflect the relative restrictiveness of each sector. Nevertheless, the indices may not be perfectly comparable across sectors. The indicators are for 2013 or the most recent year available.

Source: OECD Services Trade Restrictiveness Index (STRI)

StatLink http://dx.doi.org/10.1787/888933258541

Strengthening corporate governance

Strengthening corporate governance could reinforce efficiency, even in sectors where competitive pressures are weak. Robust corporate governance raises firm performance, in part by mitigating conflicts of interest between managers and stakeholders. State-owned and private enterprises can be held to the same high standards of transparency, governance and efficiency, even if they pursue different objectives. However, in some cases economic efficiency appears to have been sacrificed. For example, the return on equity, when taking into account state guarantees, has been negative for the main state-owned electricity company. In part, this outcome reflects past weaknesses in decision-making within the company. Basing appointments in state-owned enterprises on professional and managerial experience should be the norm, and indeed management is increasingly drawn from people with relevant experience. Another potential benefit from improving the governance of state-owned enterprise arises from levelling the playing field for the private sector.

Iceland is still implementing the OECD Anti-Bribery Convention, but progress has been slow and patchy. Making progress in its implementation and enforcement would help emphasise the government's commitment to fight corruption.

Strengthening skills on the labour market

Education, training and retraining, play an important role in ensuring that businesses can find people with the needed skills. Unfortunately, the push of lengthy school duration and the pull of demand for low-skilled workers have contributed to high dropout rates. Addressing these factors to improve high-school completion rates would strengthen the skills on the labour market.

The quality of compulsory education as measured by PISA scores is somewhat below average in Iceland, with average student performance ranking around 20th in the OECD (OECD, 2014b). The share of the population with tertiary education is also around the OECD average. However, many students drop out before finishing upper secondary education (Figure 15). Only 44% of students successfully complete upper secondary education within 4 years, against the OECD average of 68% (OECD, 2012). The consequences of a high drop-

Figure 15. **Education: Room for improvement**

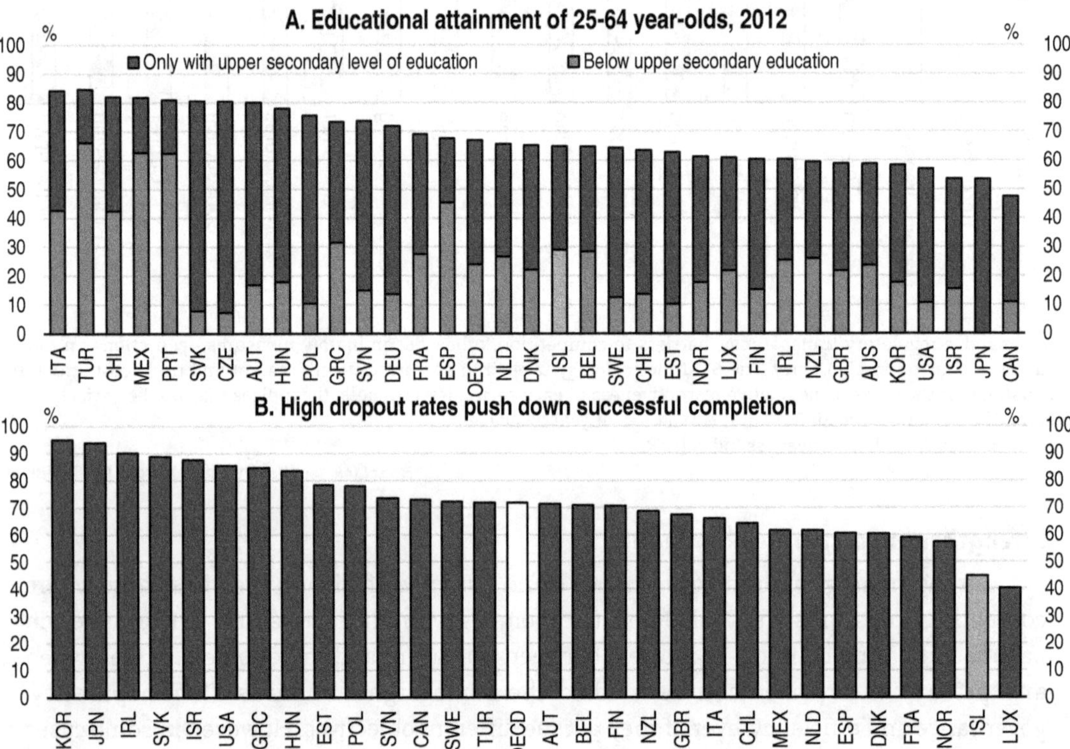

Note: Countries are ranked in descending order of the successful completion of upper secondary programmes.
Source: OECD (2014), Education at a Glance (*www.oecd.org/edu/eag.htm*).

StatLink http://dx.doi.org/10.1787/888933258555

out rate are reflected in labour market performance. While around one-third of the working-age population have only completed primary or lower secondary education, they account for the majority of those out of the labour force and nearly 45% of those unemployed. Disincentives to completing upper secondary education include the prolonged length of schooling and the late graduation age, which the *2013 OECD Economic Survey* recommended to lower. Weaknesses in vocational education and training and the pull of the labour market, particularly when pay differentials provide limited incentive to invest in skill acquisition, also act as disincentives to completing secondary education. Other factors influencing drop-out include student characteristics, such as whether the children are from immigrant families.

Against this background, the authorities reduced the length of upper-secondary schooling, allowing students to graduate a year early. Schools offering credit-based programmes have already seen markedly more pupils graduating early. Strengthening vocational education and training and supporting links with employers will increase the attractiveness of remaining in education. In addition, ensuring that all students entering secondary education are suitably prepared would help reduce drop-out rates of vulnerable groups. The recent white paper on education reform establishes two goals for 2018: increasing the graduation rate from its current rate of 44% to 60% and boosting reading literacy from 79% in 90%, which should also reduce the high school drop-out rate. The different actors involved in education (national and local authorities and teachers) need to ensure that pupils are acquiring the requisite skills as they progress through the education system (OECD, 2012).

Iceland spends more per student annually for compulsory education than the OECD average, but performs relatively poorly in attainment, as measured by PISA. The previous *Economic Survey* advocated better resource management to ensure that costs are minimised and quality increased, and efforts should continue to target higher spending efficiency in compulsory education. For example, greater guidance of attainment in the national curricula guides would allow schools and local authorities to identify where problems are emerging and make timely interventions in underperforming schools. Accompanying measures could include extending the school year, which is currently comparatively short.

An innovation in compulsory schooling that should help boost efficiency and reduce the overall length of studies is experiments with flexible transitions from compulsory schooling to upper secondary schools. These flexible transitions allow some pupils to advance to upper-secondary education early, either by taking upper-secondary school courses or enrolling in these schools. If the current evaluations of flexible transitions are favourable, these opportunities should be rolled out further.

Remuneration and the business environment

An additional channel through which productivity can be lifted is through resource reallocation towards higher productivity sectors. However, a strong degree of wage compression – often a feature in countries where union membership and bargaining coverage is high – weakens the incentives to invest in education and potentially mutes price signals that might lead to smoother resource reallocation (Figure 16). In the past, the internal rate of return on attaining upper-secondary or tertiary education has been significantly below the average in the OECD. For example, estimates reported in OECD (2006) suggest that Icelandic males enjoy less than half of the returns experienced

Figure 16. **Wages are compressed**

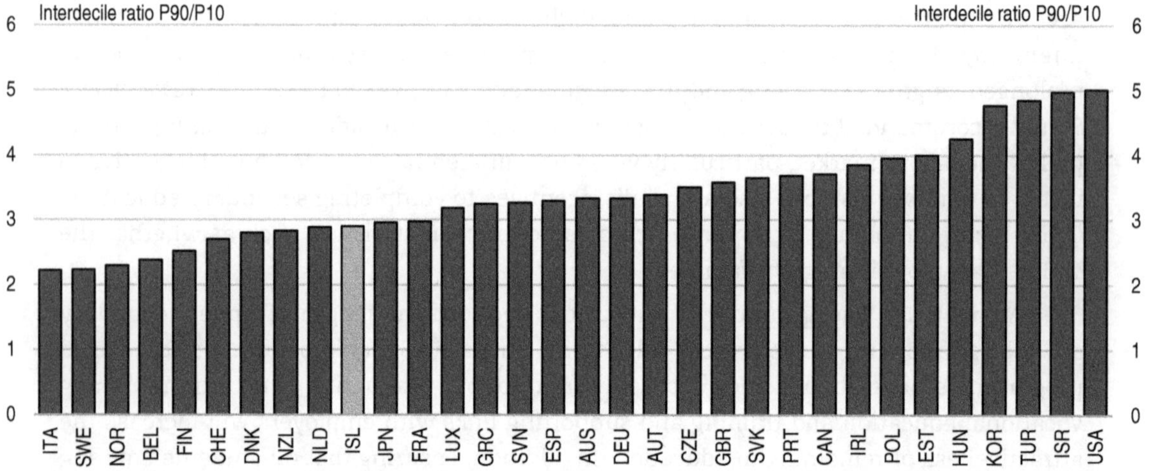

Source: OECD Labour Force Statistics – Decile ratios of gross earnings.

StatLink http://dx.doi.org/10.1787/888933258569

elsewhere. For women, returns are comparable only when they have completed tertiary education. For geographically mobile workers wage compression can also induce outmigration. With these effects there is a risk that the skills of the labour market can erode.

The distribution of wages is highly compressed by international comparison, particularly when taking into account returns to education (Statistics Iceland, 2015). In this context, a better balance needs to be struck between providing incentives for skill acquisition and resource reallocation against the possible impacts on increasing income inequality.

Using natural resources while respecting the environment

Iceland's environmental quality is generally good (OECD, 2014c). Environmental stewardship in Iceland is well developed. Indeed, in the realm of fisheries management Iceland has taken a leading role in implementing a policy framework that targets sustainability. As a member of the European Economic Area, Iceland aligns its environmental policies and legislation with that of the European Union. Nevertheless, policies have not fully addressed a number of pressures on the environment. For example, due to the fragility of the environment, over-grazing contributing to soil erosion is a major concern and has already seen a number of measures introduced. Newer challenges include ensuring that the boom in tourism is managed in a way to mitigate adverse environmental impacts, which would ultimately reduce the attractiveness of Iceland as a green tourist destination.

In recent years, the Ministry of Fisheries (now the Ministry of Industry and Innovation) has adopted the proposed total allowable catches from the scientific advisors - the Marine Research Institute – based on an assessment of catches that are consistent with fish stock sustainability. The individual transferable quota (ITQ) system, by giving participants a long-term stake in healthy fish stocks, has thereby created incentives to respect quotas and helped fish stocks recover. The flexibility in the ITQ system has also reduced overcapacity in the industry, boosting productivity. Thus while total landings of cod were almost 30% more than the total allowable catches in the initial years of the system, they have dropped to just 12% more recently and the number of fishing vessels has dropped substantially. Measures of total factor productivity in the sector have been strong and substantially higher than the fishing sectors in other Nordic countries (Eggert and Tveteras, 2013). The fisheries sector has become an important innovation cluster.

While these are positive steps, uncertainty arises in other aspects of fisheries management. Despite the system having proven very effective in managing fish resources, recent proposals could radically change the fishing regime. As the initial individual transferable quotas were allocated without charge, the owners of the fishing rights have captured resource rents as the fish stocks have recovered, fishing capacity has decreased and fish prices have risen. Levying a tax on the resource rent has allowed the government to claw back some of the rent for the broader public. Since the natural resource belongs to the Icelandic people, the resource rent should also accrue at least in part to them. Finally, a resource tax may also limit some of the pressures for Dutch disease.

Different ideas on reforms to the system have been discussed, including amending the individual transferable quotas system by introducing long-term leases to replace indefinite quotas. While details of this regime are yet to emerge, any proposal will need to ensure that sufficient incentives remain to preserve stocks and ensure economic efficiency as effectively as the current regime. For example, as fishing companies approach the termination of their lease they may be less concerned about preserving fish stocks and may stop investing, leading to losses in economic efficiency and more pronounced lumpiness in capital spending.

Reforms to the individual transferable quotas system could reconsider the carve out from the overall total allowable catch to sustain coastal communities. Over time, the ITQ share of hook and line fisheries with smaller boats has increased, but have also been captured by fewer companies and the size of the fishing vessels has grown considerably. Therefore, the original regional policy aims of this part of the carve out are not being met as effectively as before. Other parts of the carve-out include coastal fisheries with a common pool quota for small vessels and quotas allocated to vulnerable coastal communities. The rapid development of tourism as part of a broader development strategy may help sustain coastal villages without distorting the fisheries management system.

Iceland has made progress in reducing producer support for agriculture, but supports remain high by comparison with the rest of the OECD. Support continues to be applied to market prices, maintained by border measures and through direct payments, which are based on payment entitlements, directly or indirectly linked to production. From an environmental perspective, agriculture, particularly livestock grazing, can put additional burdens on the land and contribute to soil erosion and desertification. Programmes, such as the quality control programme for sheep farming, including land utilisation criteria, and Farmers Heal the Land, supporting land improvement projects, can contribute to sustainable management. Over 90% of sheep farmers participate in the quality control programme but Farmers Heal the Land has been taken up by only around one-third of sheep farmers and monitoring of the impacts on soil erosion is limited (OECD, 2014c).

Despite the abundance of hydroelectric and geothermal energy, per capita and per unit GDP emissions of greenhouse gases in Iceland are larger than the OECD average (Figure 17), though they have declined significantly. A large share of greenhouse gas emissions originate in energy-intensive industry, not from electricity generation but during

Figure 17. **GHG emissions are beginning to fall**

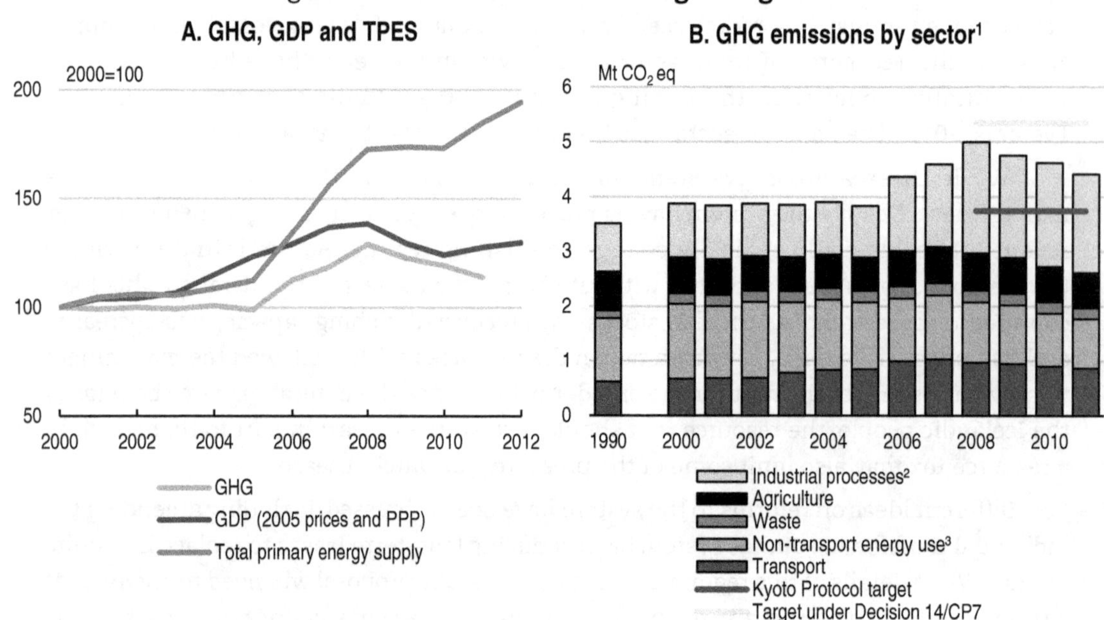

1. Excluding emissions/removals from land use, land-use change and forestry.
2. Includes solvents.
3. Includes emissions from energy use in the following sectors: manufacturing and construction; agriculture, forestry and fisheries; and residential, commercial and institutional.

Source: OECD (2013), OECD Economic Outlook No. 93 (database); UNFCCC (2013), Greenhouse Gas Inventory Data (database).

StatLink http://dx.doi.org/10.1787/888933258576

processing stages in aluminium and ferrosilicon production. Transport is the second most important source of greenhouse gas emissions. Emissions from industry have more than doubled since 1990, reflecting an allowance granted to small countries to increase emissions from some new projects if renewable energy and best available technology is used. Taking the allowance into account, greenhouse gas emissions have declined relative to the 1990 Kyoto Protocol benchmark (as emissions from a new aluminium plant are excluded) by around 4% and Iceland will have met its Kyoto-related target in the first commitment period to 2012. In a joint effort with the European Union, Iceland has communicated a target of reducing emissions by 30% by 2020 in comparison with 1990 levels, conditional on other countries setting themselves consistent targets.

The Icelandic government has already taken steps to increase abatement (Government of Iceland, 2015). For example, in 2010, a tax based on the carbon content of fuel was introduced, which unusually also covered the fishing fleet. The effective tax rate from energy use was around €76 per tonne of carbon dioxide in 2012, which was above that of the average OECD country (€50 per tonne). However, the effective tax rate varies substantially, being lower for aviation and marine fuels than for road transport fuels. As transport is the second major sources of emission, recent efforts have targeted this sector, including by changing vehicle taxation to reflect fuel efficiency and promoting renewable fuels. The impact of altering excise duties may help introduce more fuel efficient vehicles, though vehicle numbers and use may increase. In this light, taxation should adjust to price carbon emission more effectively, principally through equating marginal abatement costs across different fuels. Initiatives to use renewables or waste products as fuel for the fishing fleet and other vehicles should be expanded if current trials are successful.

Recommendations for strengthening long-term productivity growth

Main recommendations

- Adopt an ongoing productivity agenda, including following up on the priorities identified by the recent growth forum.
- Lower barriers to entry including by removing legal barriers to entry in particular sectors.
- Support innovation, including by encouraging links with universities. Ease funding access, notably with public investment funds that can finance firm expansion. Evaluate support measures.
- Toughen competition policy implementation to ensure that abuse of dominant position or cartel/tacit collusion does not stifle competition. Use the OECD's Competition Assessment Toolkit to refine law and enforcement.

Additional recommendations

- Evaluate possible ways to reduce further the length of secondary education and to lower drop-out rates.
- Harmonise marginal abatement costs in climate change policy.
- Improve monitoring of land erosion and if necessary take further action to reduce damage from sheep farming.
- Levy a resource tax on the fishing fleet and be very careful about reforming the individual transferrable quota system.
- Fully implement the OECD's Anti-Bribery convention.

Bibliography

Adalet McGowan, M. *et al.* (2015), *The Future of Productivity*, OECD Publishing, Paris.

Carcillo, S. *et al.* (2015), "NEET Youth in the Aftermath of the Crisis: Challenges and Policies", *OECD Social, Employment and Migration Working Papers*, No. 164, OECD Publishing. *http://dx.doi.org/10.1787/5js6363503f6-en*

Central Bank of Iceland (2014), *Economy of Iceland*, Central Bank of Iceland, Reykjavik.

Criscuolo, C. *et al.* (2014), "The Dynamics of Employment Growth: New Evidence from 18 countries", *OECD Science, Technology and Industry Policy Papers*, No. 14, OECD Publishing, Paris. *http://dx.doi.org/10.1787/5jz417hj6hg6-en*

Dolvik, J. *et al.* (2015), *The Nordic Model towards 2030: A New Chapter?*, Fafo, Oslo.

Eggert, H. and R. Tveteras (2013), "Productivity Development in Icelandic, Norwegian and Swedish Fisheries", *Applied Economics*, Vol. 45, No. 6, pp. 709-720.

Government of Iceland (2015), *Iceland's Sixth national Communication and First Biennial Report: under the United National Framework Convention on Climate Change*, Reykjavik.

Gylfason, T. and G. Zoega (2014), "The Dutch Disease in Reverse: Iceland's Natural Experiment", *OxCarre Research Paper*, No. 138.

Lewis, C., N. Pain, J. Strasky and F. Menkyna (2014), "Investment Gaps after the Crisis", *OECD Economics Department Working Paper*, No. 1168, OECD Publishing.

Løken, E., T Stokke and K. Nergaard (2013), "Labour Relations in Norway", *FAFO- report*, No. 2013:09.

McKinsey & Company (2012), *Charting a Growth Path for Iceland*, McKinsey Scandinavia.

Ministry of Education, Science and Culture (2014), *White Paper on Education Reform*, Reykjavik.

OECD (2004), "Chapter 3. Wage-setting Institutions and Outcomes", in *OECD Employment Outlook*, OECD Publishing, Paris.

OECD (2006), *OECD Economic Surveys: Iceland*, OECD Publishing, Paris.

OECD (2010), *Sickness, Disability and Work: Breaking the Barriers*, OECD Publishing, Paris.

OECD (2012), "Towards a Strategy to Prevent Dropout in Iceland", *Results of the OECD-Iceland Workshop Preventing Dropout in Upper Secondary Schools in Iceland*, Paris.

OECD (2013a), *OECD Economic Surveys: Iceland*, OECD Publishing, Paris.

OECD (2013b), *OECD Science, Technology and Industry Scoreboard*, OECD Publishing, Paris.

OECD (2013c), "OECD Health Data", OECD Health Statistics (Database).

OECD (2014a), *How's Life in Your Region?*, OECD Publishing, Paris.

OECD (2014b), *Education at a Glance, 2014*, OECD Publishing, Paris.

OECD (2014c), *OECD Environmental Performance Reviews: Iceland*, OECD Publishing, Paris.

OECD Competition Committee (2014), *Roundtable on Airline Competition, 18-19 June 2014: Note by Iceland*, DAF/COMP/WD(2014)45.

Statistics Iceland (2015), "Iceland has the smallest educational related income gap in Europe", *http://www.statice.is/Pages/444?NewsID=11774*

ANNEX

Progress in structural reform

The objective of this Annex is to review action taken since the previous Survey (June 2013) on the main recommendations from previous Surveys, which are not reviewed and assessed in the current Survey.

Economic rebalancing

Main recent OECD recommendations	Actions taken since the 2013 Survey
Continue to tighten monetary policy as activity recovers to reduce inflation to the target rate and anchor inflation expectations.	Inflation has come down closer to the Central Bank's target of 2.5% but inflation expectations do not appear to be firmly anchored.
Focus household debt relief on households in financial stress to reduce default risk most effectively.	The Debt Relief Programme enacted in 2014 was available to all mortgage holders; the government did not focus its actions on the most financially distressed households.
Replace the mortgage interest tax deduction by housing cost subsidies for low-income households to further reduce financial stress, reduce the bias towards owner-occupied housing and enhance equity	No action taken.
Remove the government repayment guarantee for the HFF once household finances return to good health to reduce incentives for household leverage.	No action taken.
Continue to apply high capital adequacy risk weightings on nonperforming business loans to maintain pressure on banks to write-off or restructure them.	High capital ratios have been maintained effectively and pressure from the competition authority required banks to restructure nonperforming loans.

Capital controls, monetary policy framework and financial stability

Main recent OECD recommendations	Actions taken since the 2013 Survey
Macro-prudential policies, such as maximum loan-to-value ratios or cyclically varying loan-loss provisioning requirements, should be used to mitigate risks to financial stability, dampen credit cycles and complement monetary policy.	No action taken but the government is in the process of introducing similar measures.
Proceed with the established programme for removal of the capital controls at a pace that is conditioned upon economic developments.	The authorities have made progress in preparing for the removal of capital controls. Elements of a plan have not been finalised.
Once capital controls are lifted, maintain an inflation targeting framework for monetary policy with a floating exchange rate. A heightened emphasis on exchange rate stability is warranted, but limits the scope of currency market interventions to smoothing erratic fluctuations.	Capital controls are still in place.
Strengthen co-ordination and communication between financial sector supervisory authorities.	Achieved.
Establish an explicit mandate for maintaining financial stability that clearly defines responsibility and gives supervisors the statutory authority and instruments to carry out their responsibilities.	Partially achieved: the mandate has been established but the authorities still do not have all the necessary instruments.

Fiscal consolidation

Main recent OECD recommendations	Actions taken
Take immediate action to ensure that the budget remains on track to reach balance in 2014 and a surplus of 2% of GDP by 2015 to put public debt on a path to more prudent levels.	Partially achieved: the budget has achieved balance in 2014 but there is no sign of a surplus of 2% of GDP by 2015. However, debt is on a path to more prudent levels.
Focus fiscal consolidation measures on current expenditures to increase the likelihood that consolidation is sustained and to make room for a return to stronger infrastructure investment.	Achieved. Current spending has declined as a share of GDP and the 2015 budget increased infrastructure investment.
To increase transparency and credibility, adopt a timeline for debt reduction with intermediate targets.	Partially achieved: the Ministry of Finance and Economic Affairs has published the government's Medium-term Debt Management Strategy for the period 2014-2017 and the Fiscal Plan for 2016-2019: However, the plans do not include a detailed timeline with intermediate targets.
Pass the proposed Organic Budget Law to strengthen budget discipline.	Not achieved but currently under consideration in the parliament.

Government expenditure efficiency

Main recent OECD recommendations	Actions taken
Undertake strategic spending reviews to seek potential efficiency gains and reorient expenditure towards government priorities.	No action taken.
To reduce costs and increase returns to education, reduce the duration of primary and secondary education.	Partially achieved: the authorities acted to reduce the length of upper-secondary schooling, allowing students to graduate a year early.
Strengthen gate-keeping in health care to reduce specialist consultations, guide patients to more appropriate care and reduce examinations using expensive diagnostic equipment. As this would raise GP workloads, increase funding for GPs	No action taken.

Green growth

Main recent OECD recommendations	Actions taken
Broaden the base for the carbon tax and raise its rate to increase cost-effective abatement of GHG emissions.	Partially achieved: a carbon tax was introduced in 2010 and levied on liquid fossil fuels, electricity consumption and hot water. Its base has not been broadened to non-liquid carbon–based fuels and rates were not raised. Iceland joined the EU-ETS, but the impact of the trading system has been limited in Iceland.
Develop exported electricity capacity (notably through energy-intensive industries) if long-run marginal costs (including the return on capital) are fully covered. If there are resource rents, tax them.	No action taken.
Reduce the scheduled increases in the special fisheries resource rent tax to levels that the industry can cope with, especially in the demersal sector.	Achieved.

Thematic chapters

Chapter 1

A policy framework to promote stability and resilience

Iceland's openness to global capital and goods markets has contributed to fast-rising living standards over the past decades. Nonetheless, its unusual status as a very small open economy with an independent currency has left the country susceptible to macroeconomic instability. The banking sector's collapse of 2008 and 2009 was the latest example, when financial turbulence from abroad was amplified by serious shortcomings in domestic policy. Countries can promote stability without resorting to capital controls or exchange-rate pegs by implementing well-designed frameworks for monetary policy, fiscal policy and financial regulation. In addition, resilience to destabilising capital flows can be bolstered by maintaining precautionary buffers, notably substantial holdings of foreign exchange reserves, as well as ample bank capital buffers and fiscal space.

Promoting stability and improving resilience without capital controls

Iceland's history amply demonstrates that financial instability can inflict large damages. Following the latest episode in October 2008, the unemployment rate climbed nearly 8 percentage points, per capita consumption fell nearly 20%, and the sovereign risk premium spiked dramatically (see Einarsson *et al.*, 2015). More broadly, the boom-bust cycle prompted a costly reshuffling of resources from the tradable sector to the non-tradable sector and back (Figure 1.1). This was only the latest in a series of sizeable cyclical swings (Figure 1.2).

Figure 1.1. **The financial boom and its aftermath reshuffled resources between sectors**

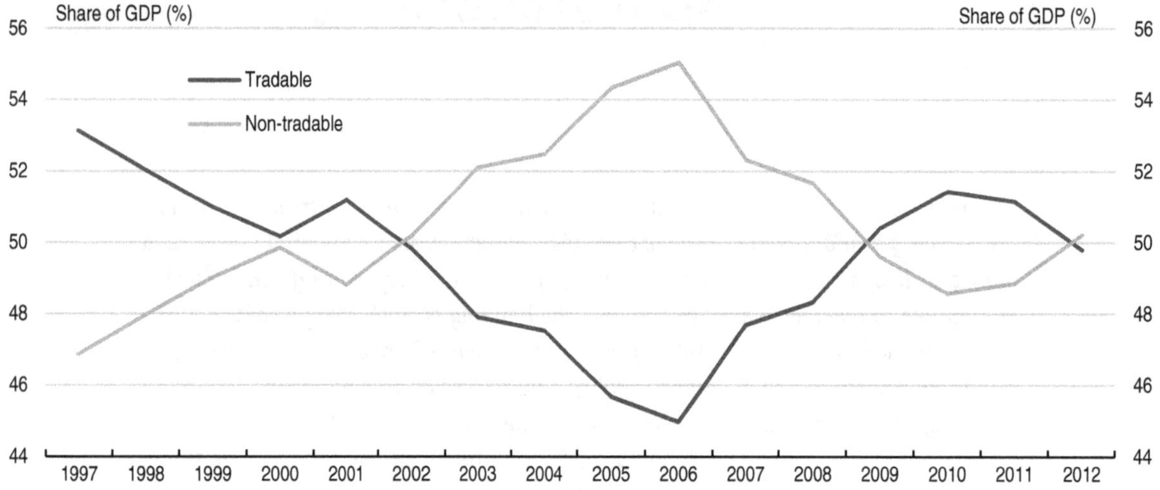

Note: Tradables include Agriculture, forestry and fishing; Mining and quarrying; Manufacturing; Wholesale and retail trade; repair of motor vehicles and motorcycles; Transportation and storage; Financial and insurance activities and Professional, scientific and technical activities. All other categories are considered non-tradables.
Source: Statistics Iceland and OECD calculations.

StatLink http://dx.doi.org/10.1787/888933258585

After the collapse of the three largest domestic banks, the government enacted capital account controls to stem currency outflows and forestall further depreciation of the exchange rate. These controls restricted foreign currency transactions between residents and non-residents involving cross-border capital movements. Although current account transactions were generally exempted, domestic residents were obliged to repatriate into domestic banks foreign currency proceeds from current account transactions. New investments were exempted from the rules in late 2009 (Central Bank of Iceland, 2010), and subsequent amendments tightened supervision, eliminated loopholes, imposed heftier penalties for violations, and granted authority to the central bank to control distributions from the failed banks' estates.

Originally these controls were expected to be in place for a limited period, but they are still in force. The main impediment to lifting them is the concern that this would unleash

Figure 1.2. **Business cycles produce considerable swings in economic outcomes**

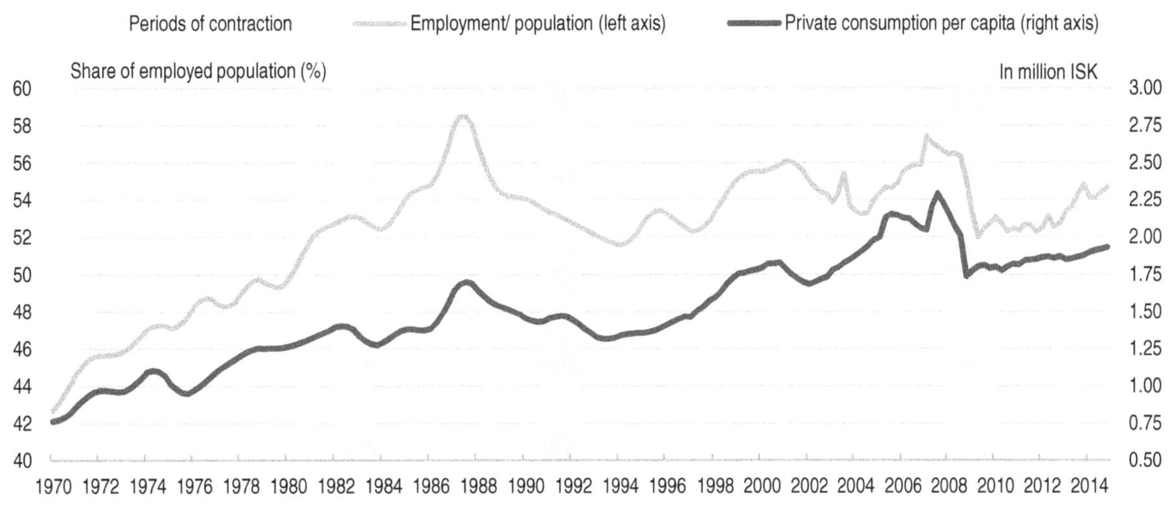

Source: OECD Analytical database and Central Bank of Iceland (contraction periods).

StatLink http://dx.doi.org/10.1787/888933258593

large and disruptive capital outflows. It has been estimated that Iceland's "balance of payments overhang"—that is, the net outflow of króna that would eventually be needed to bring domestic and foreign asset holdings to desired levels—amounted to 70% of GDP in late 2014 (IMF, 2015b). Iceland has only recently formulated comprehensive plans to address this threat, in part because of the problem's complexity.

Although capital controls contradict Iceland's international commitments with the OECD, EEA and other organizations, these bodies agreed that the threat to stability was sufficient to satisfy provisions allowing for a temporary suspension (Box 1.1 discusses Iceland's OECD obligations). This decision was motivated by concerns that pass-through to inflation from further deterioration in the króna would have had destructive balance-sheet effects, in part because most home mortgage loans were inflation indexed. The controls seemingly forestalled these effects: the króna quickly stabilised and has remained stable, while monetary policy has managed to rein in inflation from its peak of near 20% in early 2009.

Box 1.1. **Iceland's status under the OECD Codes of Liberalisation**

In March 2011, Iceland invoked the derogation clause under Article 7(b) of the OECD Codes of Liberalisation of Capital Movements for reasons of serious economic and financial disturbance (OECD, 2011). The Investment Committee agreed that Iceland's invocation was justified in light of the serious disturbance to the country's financial system, and the OECD Council endorsed this conclusion while encouraging Iceland to remove the restrictions as soon as progress in strengthening the financial system would allow. The derogation has provided Iceland with flexibility to respond to the crisis and ongoing dialogue has allowed Iceland to obtain international support and keep Code adherents informed about progress and measures taken.

The Advisory Task Force on the OECD Codes of Liberalisation and Current Invisible Operations (ATFC) last reviewed Iceland's derogation on April 22, 2015. Iceland has been asked to provide periodic notifications to the OECD regarding progress in lifting its derogation, and the ATFC will revisit the case later in 2015.

Unrestricted capital flows can entail heightened financial risks and occasional instability for small countries such as Iceland, contributing to domestic credit booms, asset price bubbles, and exposures of domestic balance sheets to foreign currency risks (e.g. Reinhart and Reinhart, 2008, Barajas *et al.*, 2007). Such susceptibilities often arise because private agents take excessive risks that fail to internalise the overall effect of their actions on financial market stability (Korinek, 2011). There is an emerging consensus that prudential measures can help resolve such market failures, reducing the incidence and severity of financial crises in a way that tends to enhance overall welfare. This contention seems broadly consistent with existing empirical evidence (IMF, 2012a; Ostry *et al.*, 2010, 2011, and 2012), and the IMF, for example, recognises the potential destabilising effects of capital flows can justify measures to manage them. That said, the IMF continues to recommend that Iceland's capital restrictions be lifted as soon as macroeconomic conditions allow (IMF, 2015b).

The controls were successful in the sense of allowing Iceland to sidestep a much deeper economic contraction and to achieve a more rapid economic recovery than other countries hard hit by the crisis (Figure 1.3). Controls freed up monetary policy to lower interest rates to stimulate domestic activity rather than support the currency, while trapped domestic savings helped insulate the banks from funding risk, supported domestic asset prices, and facilitated private and public deleveraging.

However, controls also likely generate negative side effects. Capital flow restrictions reduce economic efficiency by undermining the role of prices in directing resources toward their highest-valued use. This inefficiency occurs, in part, through a mispricing of risk, as lack of access to international markets undermines international risk sharing and distorts domestic asset prices. Investment may also be delayed by uncertainty about both the resolution of the current controls and the possibility that they may someday be re-imposed. Financial openness and FDI are found to have a positive impact on productivity and economic growth (Kose *et al.*, 2008), while capital controls appear to exert various negative effects such as more costly and less efficient financial services (especially for small firms), diminished financial market discipline, and deadweight losses from attempts to evade restrictions.

Figure 1.3. **Iceland is recovering comparatively strongly**

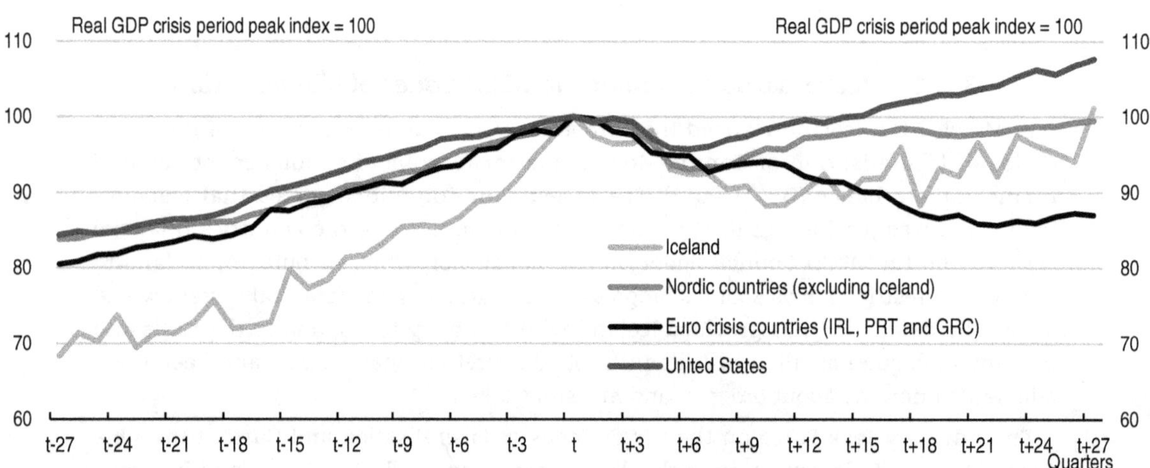

Note: Peak quarter is 2007Q4 for the Nordic countries and Ireland, 2008Q1 for Portugal, 2007Q2 for Greece and 2008Q2 for the United States.

Source: OECD Analytical database and OECD calculations.

StatLink http://dx.doi.org/10.1787/888933258411

Evidence suggests that such distortions are occurring in Iceland. Although offshore trading of the króna is thin, the currency trades abroad at a significant discount relative to the official domestic rate (Figure 1.4), consistent with sizeable effects on the terms of trade. Even though the capital controls exempt new investment, incoming FDI has remained modest relative to precrisis norms, in part due to uncertainties and perceived costs of obtaining approvals. Icelandic businesses single out foreign-currency regulations as the single most important impediment to doing business (World Economic Forum, 2015), and start-ups complain about being held back by uncertainty, as well as by a lack of foreign capital and expertise. The controls have also forced domestic pension funds to channel contributions toward domestic assets rather than taking advantage of international risk sharing, which may be laying the seeds for future instability (Figure 1.5). The weight of such

Figure 1.4. **The króna has been trading at a discount in offshore markets**

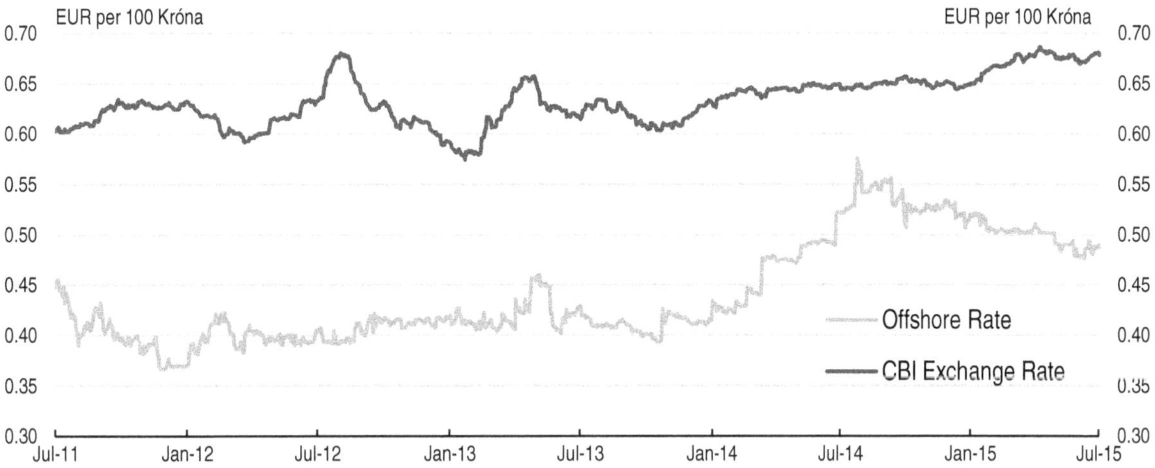

EUR per 100 Króna

Offshore Rate

CBI Exchange Rate

Jul-11, Jan-12, Jul-12, Jan-13, Jul-13, Jan-14, Jul-14, Jan-15, Jul-15

Source: Datastream.

StatLink http://dx.doi.org/10.1787/888933258608

Figure 1.5. **Capital controls have pushed down pension funds' foreign asset holdings**

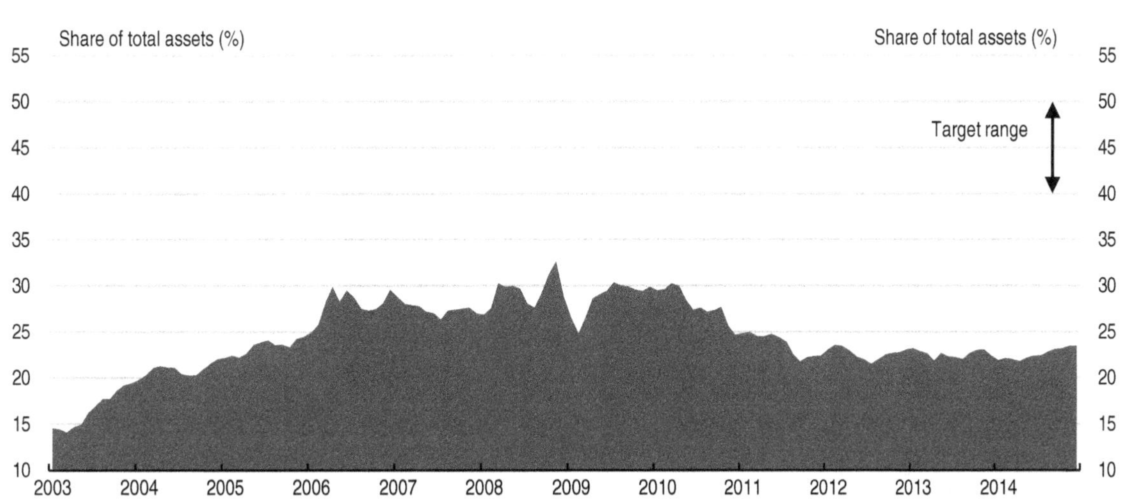

Source: Icelandic Pension Funds Association.

StatLink http://dx.doi.org/10.1787/888933258619

distortions on economic growth in Iceland will become more apparent with the economy returning to full employment.

The road forward

The Icelandic authorities recognise that the controls are harmful to longer-term economic prospects and have been working to ensure that a more robust financial stability framework and other buffers are in place when the controls are lifted. However, a precondition for any liberalisation strategy will be to rein in the balance of payments overhang. Even with bolstered financial defenses, lifting the controls could unleash capital outflows that would place renewed downward pressure on the króna and precipitate further economic distress.

In 2011, the authorities outlined a liberalisation plan that envisioned first channelling offshore króna (which are mainly the legacy of carry trade funds trapped in Iceland in 2008) to longer-term investors until their level became manageable relative to official reserve holdings. This initial measure would pave the way for a second stage where controls would be gradually lifted provided that conditions were in place to minimise financial disruptions, such as a trade outlook sufficient to accommodate likely net capital outflows, a financial sector resilient enough to withstand volatile capital flows, and prudential rules to forestall foreign exchange risk (Central Bank of Iceland, 2014a). The lifting was to be supported, if necessary, by exit taxes or other measures designed to slow capital outflows. The CBI has enacted the first stage of this plan by conducting periodic auctions in which foreign investors wishing to offload short-term króna assets are paired with investors wishing to purchase longer-term domestic securities (such as Treasuries and approved private-sector assets) with foreign currency. These auctions, combined with and other measures, have pared the stock of foreign-held short-term króna assets from about 40% of annual GDP in 2008 to just 15% of GDP in December 2014 (Figure 1.6, left panel).

Figure 1.6. **Offshore króna holdings remain large in relation to GDP**

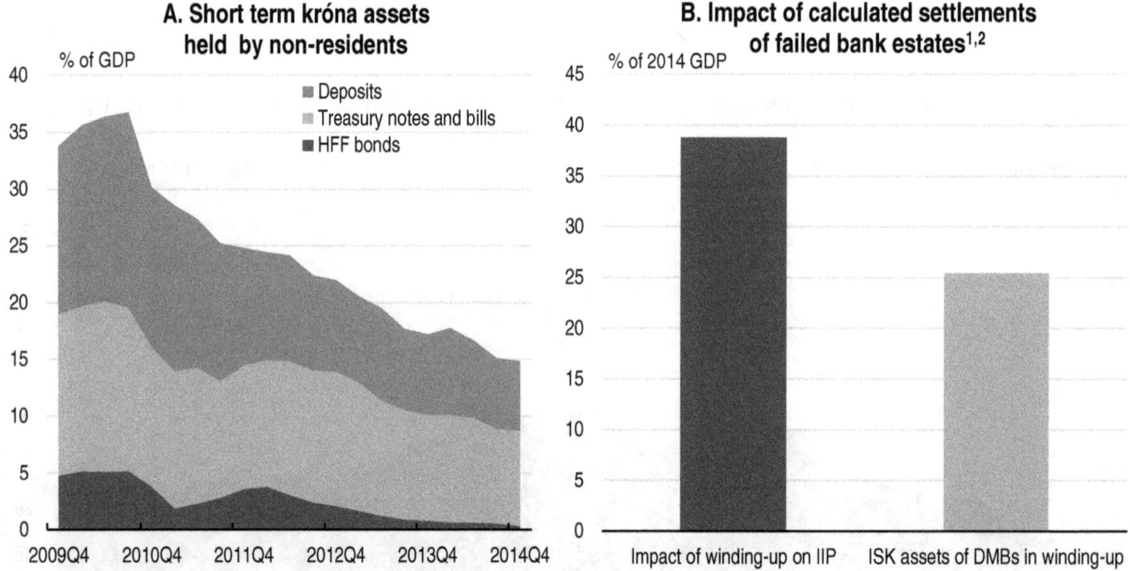

1. Book value of assets 31 December 2014.
2. Assuming equal distribution of assets among creditors; no consideration is given to future tax payments or other issues pertaining to the settlement of the estates.

Sources: Statistics Iceland, Central Bank of Iceland and claims lists and financial information Glitnir, Kaupthing and LBI.

StatLink http://dx.doi.org/10.1787/888933258629

Even so, the 2011 plan became inadequate as new information revealed the magnitude of the overhang tied to the insolvent bank estates. These estates are what remains of the failed banks after the government carved out their domestic deposits and loan portfolios to salvage a domestic banking system. To compensate for this carve out, the government granted each estate claims on the bank that succeeded it, including bonds issued by the new Landsbanki and equity stakes in the two other new banks, Arion and Íslandbanki. But this carve-out occurred under difficult and uncertain conditions and—with the relative boost to domestic asset values from the stronger-than-expected recovery—the estates were left with a substantial imbalance between foreign assets (59% of total value) and foreign claims (96% of total value). The authorities extended the controls to cover the estates in March 2012 once the sizeable net capital outflow that would occur if these positions were unwound became apparent. A comparatively small amount of assets were also trapped in some failed savings banks.

At the end of 2014, remaining assets in these three estates had a book value equivalent to 112% of GDP (Figure 1.7). Króna-denominated domestic assets in the three estates account for about 23% of this value (25% of GDP) and would pose the most direct threat to the domestic currency if distributed (Figure 1.6, right panel). The remaining assets are foreign currency denominated, including liquid instruments in Iceland (7% of GDP) and abroad (47% of GDP) that could be distributed with no direct balance of payments implications, as well as other assets (such as loans) that could pose risks in cases where the borrower lacks foreign currency resources to fund payments. For example, even though payments on the Landsbankinn bonds are denominated in foreign exchange, they pose a threat to the balance of payments (and risks to the creditworthiness of Landsbankinn more generally) because the new bank's foreign currency inflows are insufficient to fund these payments internally. An agreement reached in late 2014 greatly diminished these risks, as payments originally scheduled on these bonds from 2015 to 2018 were extended through 2026. To compensate for this extension, the Landsbanki estate was granted exemptions

Figure 1.7. **Composition of the failed banks' assets**

Book value of assets as a percentage of annual GDP, 31 December 2014

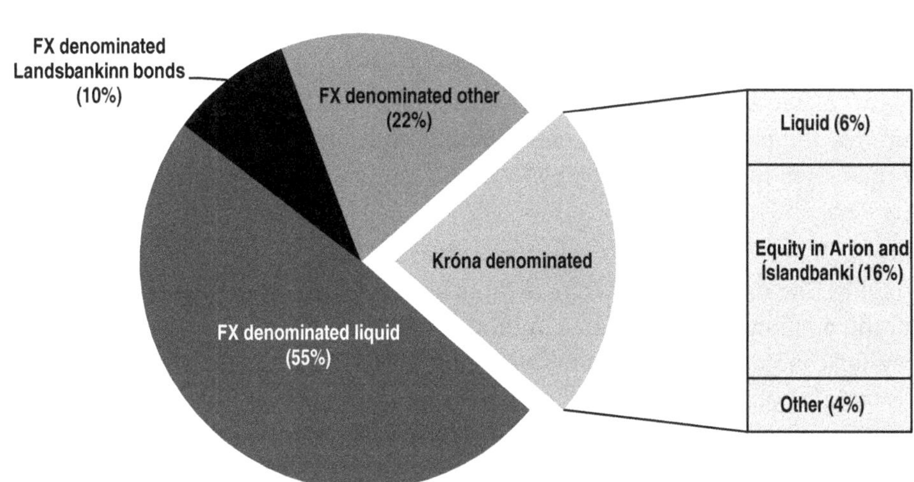

Source: Central Bank of Iceland.

that authorised it to release liquid foreign currency assets amounting to 20% of GDP to priority claimholders (including claims originating from earlier pay-outs by deposit insurance programmes in the Netherlands and the United Kingdom). With this agreement, nearly all of the estates' priority claims have been repaid.

Rebalancing of domestic pension fund assets has also emerged as a balance of payments vulnerability. These funds, whose assets amount to nearly 150% of GDP, eventually intend to boost foreign asset holdings from their current share of 22% to between 40% and 50% when they regain access to international asset markets, which could unleash a capital outflow as large as 40% of GDP. Although such diversification is highly desirable, its timing will require careful management.

In June 2015, the authorities announced a new plan to unwind the failed banks and the remaining offshore króna, which was formed in consultation with a task force of outside experts (including economists and international legal experts) appointed by the government in July 2014. Successfully implementing this plan would reduce substantially Iceland's balance of payment overhang by roughly half of its current 70% level relative to GDP as estimated by the IMF.

The plan is designed to encourage the winding up boards of the three largest estates to negotiate composition agreements and measures amongst the creditors that would allocate remaining assets in a way that satisfies specified stability conditions, including:

- taking measures to defuse the threat from distributing their króna-denominated assets, such as making an offsetting "stability contribution" to the authorities;
- extending the maturity of foreign-currency denominated domestic assets (such as foreign exchange bank deposits) to terms of 7 to 10 years; and
- refinancing or otherwise ensuring repayment of foreign-exchange denominated loans granted by the authorities to the new banks following the crisis.

Estates that fail to reach suitable composition plans by the end of 2015 would be subject to a one-time "stability tax" (payable in króna) on their total asset holdings of 39% — roughly in line with the proportion of all domestic assets in the three estates (króna denominated or otherwise). The failed savings banks would pay this tax as well. Banks can reduce their tax to an average effective rate of around 32% by converting liquid domestic foreign-currency holdings into longer-term assets. The tax is calibrated to generate enough revenue to offset any potential risk of capital outflows from unwinding the insolvent institutions, thereby encouraging creditors to voluntarily propose and implement less costly measures to neutralise their effects on the balance of payments and financial stability.

Although the legislation is subject to litigation risk, the response thus far has been encouraging. The major creditors of the three largest estates have already proposed plans that, in the opinion of the task force, fulfil the stability conditions. These plans may pave the way for composition agreements and exemptions from the capital controls for the three estates by year-end. Each proposal still requires approval from estate claimholders representing at least 60% of the claimants and between 60% and 90% of the total value of claims (depending on write-offs). The government estimates that stability contributions by the estates would temporarily raise its revenues by between 18% and 32% of 2014 GDP, compared to a boost between 34% and 42% of GDP if the stability tax is assessed on the estates. In either case, the government intends to channel the proceeds to align with economic and financial stability objectives.

To resolve the overhang of remaining offshore króna, authorities plan to hold a one-time auction that will give investors the choice of converting their funds to either longer-term government bonds (denominated in króna or foreign exchange) or to foreign exchange at a cost. Unconverted funds will be locked in non-interest bearing accounts for a lengthy period, thereby discouraging holdouts.

The authorities have also recently announced capital flow exemptions that will allow pension funds to make foreign asset purchases over the remainder of 2015 amounting to as much as ½ percent of GDP. Exemptions will be allocated amongst applicants according to their size (weighting 70%) and net inflows (weighting 30%). In order to facilitate further portfolio rebalancing, it would be sensible for the central bank to continue to set limits on the flow of foreign asset purchases in light of balance of payments pressures. Adjustments to these limits could also serve as a tool to help lean against destabilising capital flows.

The Icelandic authorities should continue to ensure that their measures abide by their obligations under various international agreements, which should help minimise any adverse impacts of the plan on the credibility of the government's future commitment to property rights and free capital flows. The authorities are working with the OECD's Investment Committee and its Advisory Task Force to ensure that their plans abide by the Codes of Liberalisation of Capital Movements and Current Invisible Operations.

Once the plan to address the overhang has been fully implemented, the authorities will be in a position to begin gradually lifting capital controls. Depending on the outcome of the plan and potential litigation delays, this process could begin as early as mid-2016. Although this process will involve risks, it is expected to be reinforced by supportive fundamentals for the króna. Icelandic trade surpluses have been averaging about 8% of GDP per year since 2009, driven in part by ongoing government consolidation that has freed up domestic savings, a low real exchange rate, and a reorientation of production toward tradable goods. Although cost pressures from the generous recent wage settlements are projected to reduce these surpluses, pressures to generate such large surpluses should diminish due to the anticipated reduction in the balance of payments overhang (Figure 1.8). Financial imbalances have also faded, as consolidation in the government and private sectors has boosted confidence in the sustainability of domestic debt, and the financial sector has been shored up by selling assets, bolstered capital reserves, and new prudential instruments. With inflationary pressures mounting and full employment approaching, monetary policy is projected to enter a tightening cycle that should also help attract foreign capital inflows in the face of very low projected interest rates abroad.

Even so, reopening the economy to capital flows will also re-expose the economy's vulnerabilities that precipitated the crisis. A resilient policy environment needs to be in place to help manage potential risks and instil confidence in future stability. Important work is still needed behind the scenes to ensure that a transparent and robust financial framework is in place that promotes macroeconomic stability and that actively inhibits the accumulation of financial imbalances, with sufficient buffers to reinforce the system and strengthen confidence. The remaining sections of this chapter sketch an outline for such a framework.

Figure 1.8. **Iceland's international investment position has improved markedly**

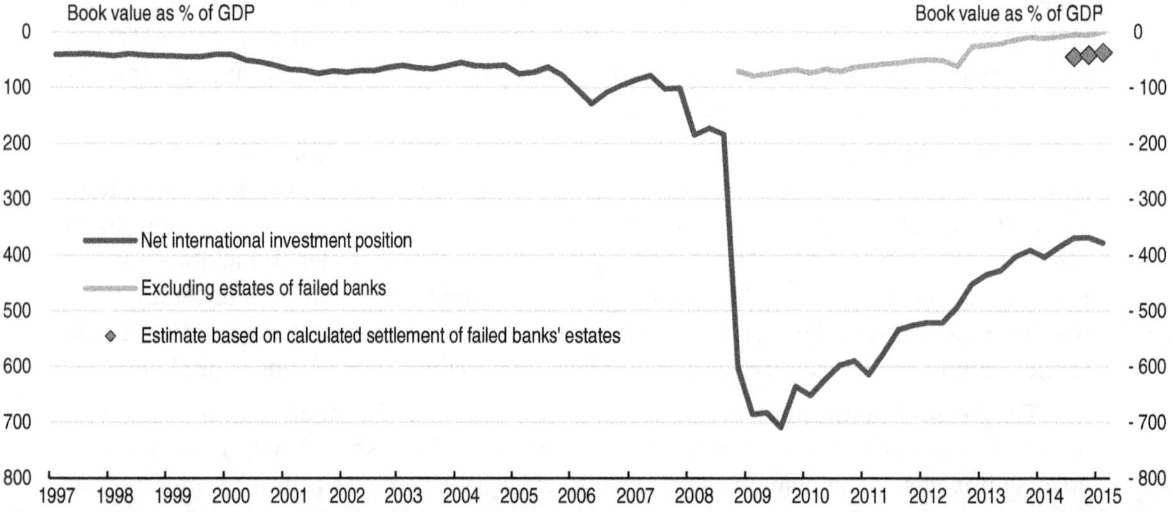

Note: Net position includes failed banks' estates, whose external liabilities well exceed remaining assets (external and domestic). These losses will go almost entirely to external creditors. Calculated settlement assumes that the estates' remaining assets are allocated to stakeholders in line with registered claims.

Source: OECD Analytical database and Central Bank of Iceland.

StatLink http://dx.doi.org/10.1787/888933258637

Monetary policy after the removal of capital controls

Domestic monetary policy outcomes have been mixed since the Central Bank of Iceland was established in 1961 (Central Bank of Iceland, 2010). Despite experiments with fixed and floating exchange rate over its history, average annual inflation rates (measured by percent changes in the harmonised CPI) have been at the upper end of the OECD range (Figure 1.9). The variability of inflation and output growth has also been very high in comparison to other OECD countries (Figure 1.10), but inflation variability has diminished substantially since 1990 (see Central Bank of Iceland, 2014d). Since the crisis, inflation has declined, on balance, to levels in line with the OECD average, and inflationary expectations are gradually following suit. Sustaining these declines would benefit the Icelandic economy by reducing impediments to resource allocation from distorted price signals, uncertainty, and high risk premia.

Many considerations make monetary policy implementation particularly challenging in Iceland, and these influences will likely re-intensify after capital controls are lifted. The economy is exposed to frequent fluctuations in the terms of trade from international capital flows and global price movements (see Einarsson *et al.*, 2015). This exposure is magnified by the country's small size and by the limited diversity of its exports, which are concentrated in products that derive from a handful of natural resources, such as marine products and renewable energy. In addition, the high import share of consumer spending (about 35%) and poorly anchored inflation expectations make consumer prices sensitive to pass through from fluctuations in the value of the króna (Figure 1.11). According to estimates by the CBI (2008), the effect on CPI inflation from an exogenous 10% trade-weighted depreciation of the króna peaks at an increase of about 1¼ percent after one year and then diminishes to zero at horizons of two years or longer. The cumulative pass-through to the price level is about 4% (Pétursson, 2010) – roughly four times the average for the six largest OECD economies.

Figure 1.9. **Icelandic inflation has generally been high**

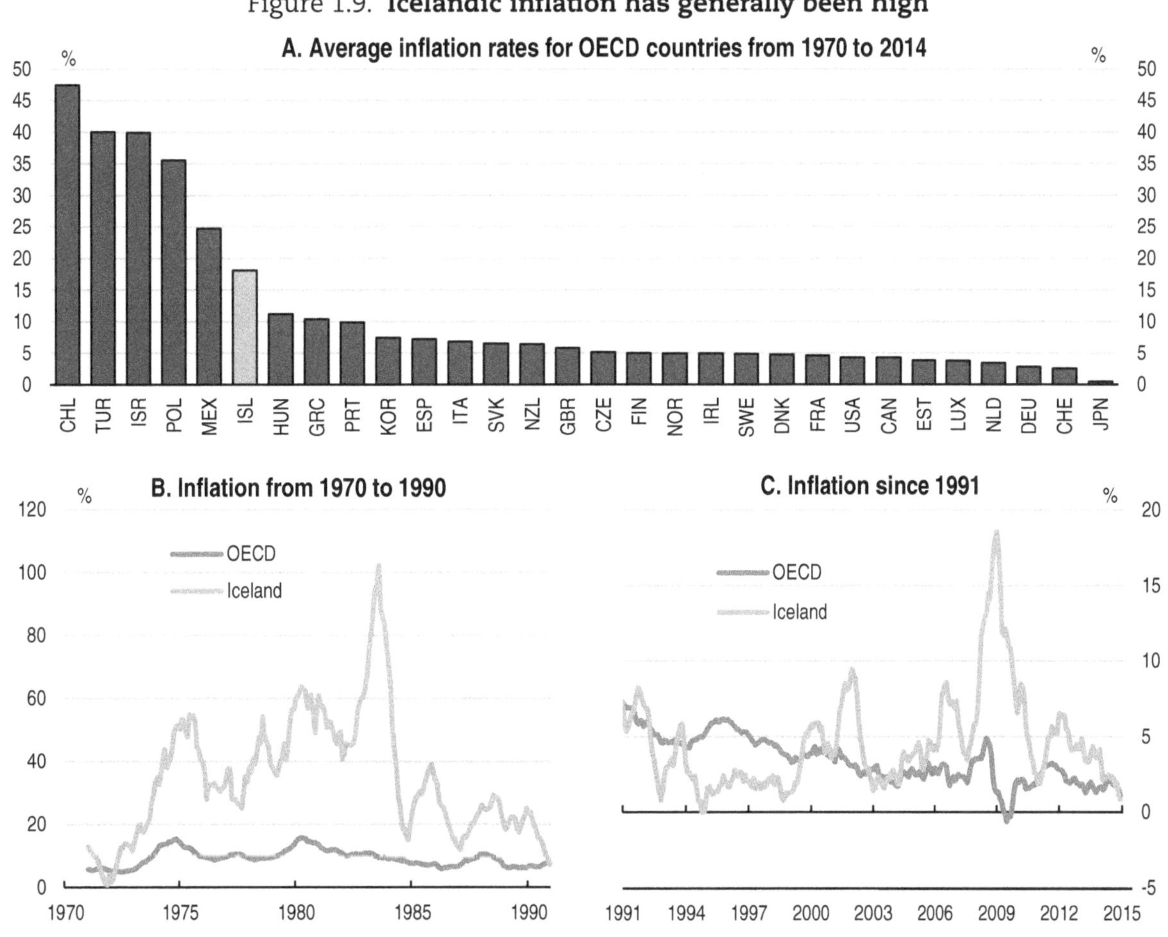

Source: OECD Analytical database and Main Economic Indicators database.

StatLink http://dx.doi.org/10.1787/888933258642

Monetary transmission channels have been compromised at times by residents taking out loans in foreign currency to sidestep attempts to tighten financial conditions (Figure 1.12). More generally, the tendency for rising króna interest rates to generate carry trades made the CBI at times hesitant to tighten policy, as this would generate further capital inflows and mounting financial system imbalances. Similarly, Iceland has also long been susceptible to asset price bubbles and financial accelerator effects, which can feed instabilities in the financial system that pose dilemmas for monetary policy. Effectiveness has also been undermined by unexpected pro-cyclical fiscal policy actions, political pressures, and wage settlements that can bear little resemblance to underlying fundamentals.

Notwithstanding these challenges, the root cause of Iceland's poor inflation record rests ultimately with monetary policy. In trade-weighted terms, the external value of the króna has depreciated steadily, and now stands at less than 1% of where it had stood in 1970. Inflation dropped significantly following agreements that reduced wage indexation and de-emphasised the government's frequent reliance on the central bank as a source of funding (OECD, 1991), and the trade-weighted value of the króna changed little, on balance, between 1991 and early 2001. However, like many small countries, Iceland's exchange rate peg regime gradually became unworkable over this period in the face of intensifying

Figure 1.10. **Macroeconomic outcomes have been comparatively volatile**

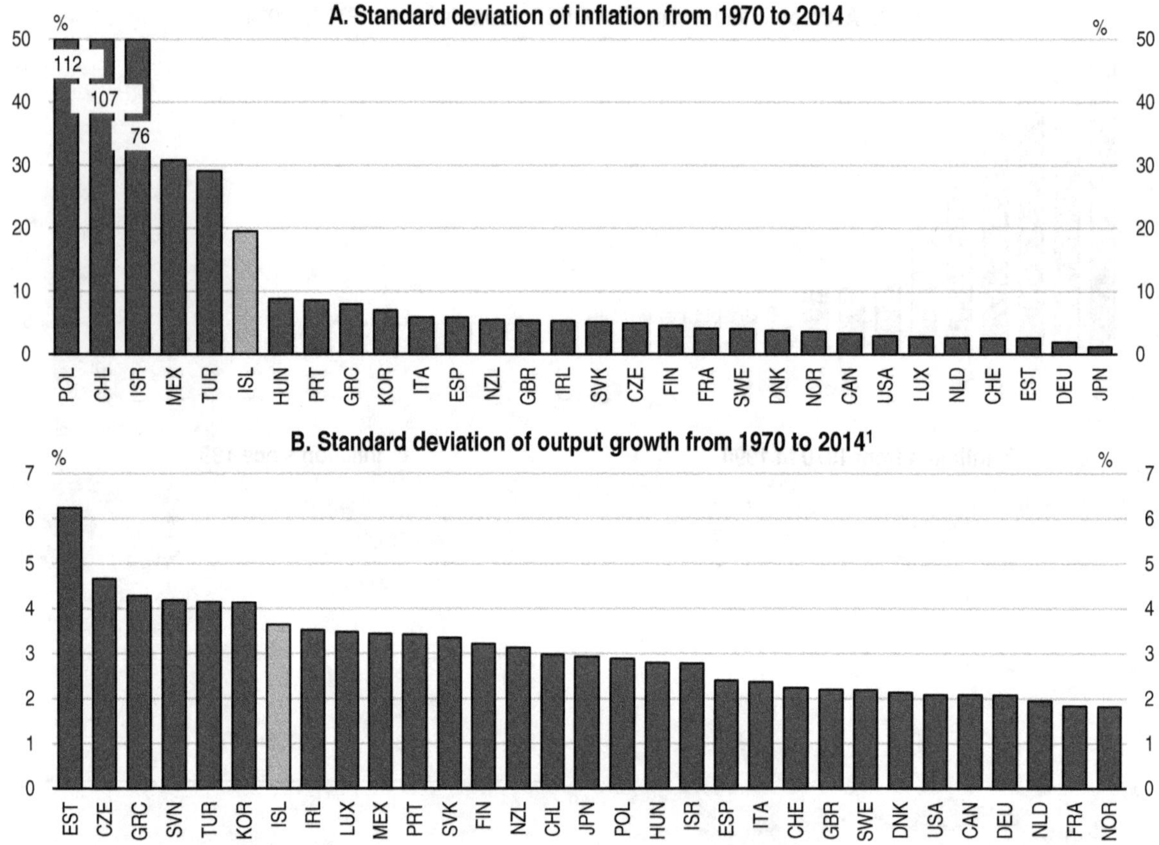

A. Standard deviation of inflation from 1970 to 2014

%

112 107 76

POL CHL ISR MEX TUR ISL HUN PRT GRC KOR ITA ESP NZL GBR IRL SVK CZE FIN FRA SWE DNK NOR CAN USA LUX NLD CHE EST DEU JPN

B. Standard deviation of output growth from 1970 to 2014[1]

%

EST CZE GRC SVN TUR KOR ISL IRL LUX MEX PRT SVK FIN NZL CHL JPN POL HUN ISR ESP ITA CHE GBR SWE DNK USA CAN DEU NLD FRA NOR

1. Real GDP volatility is measured as the standard deviation of GDP growth from 1970 to 2014.

Source: OECD Analytical database.

StatLink http://dx.doi.org/10.1787/888933258652

Figure 1.11. **Inflation is sensitive to fluctuations in the króna exchange rate**

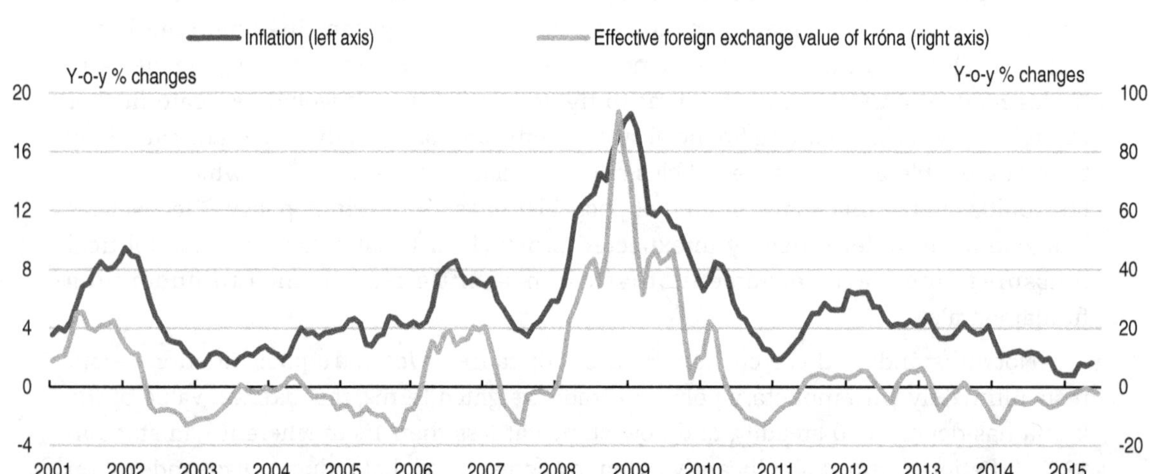

Source: OECD Analytical database and Central Bank of Iceland

StatLink http://dx.doi.org/10.1787/888933258668

Figure 1.12. **Domestic foreign exchange borrowing surged before the crisis**

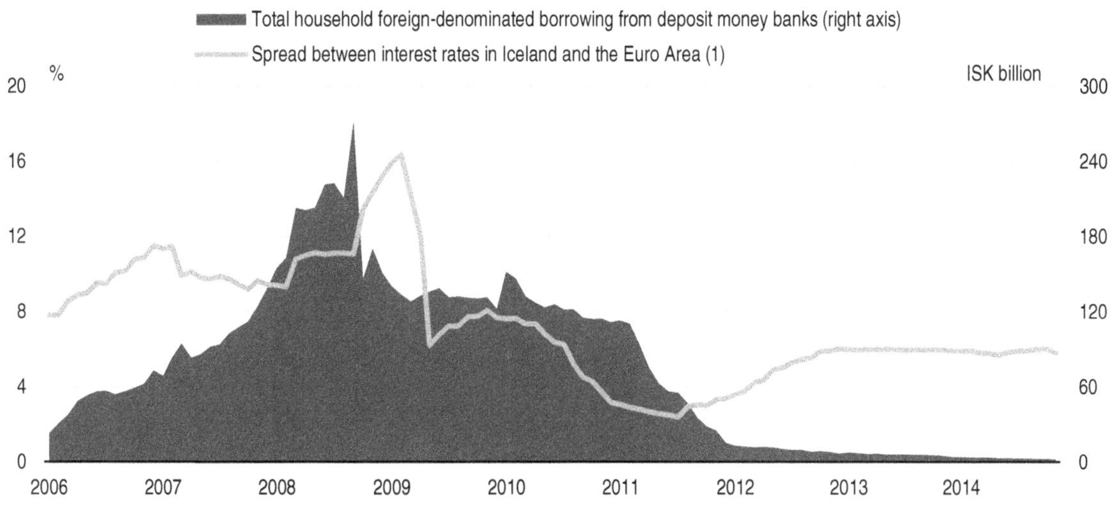

1. Three-month interbank rates.
Source: Statistics Iceland, Datastream.

StatLink http://dx.doi.org/10.1787/888933258679

pressures from capital market liberalisation and the increasing sophistication of financial markets. In 2001, a new central bank statute switched to an explicit price stability objective as well codifying the goal of promoting a sound financial system. Although the statute allows the definition of price stability to be changed by agreement with the Minister of Finance, this objective has thus far been implemented as an inflation target (IT) that has aimed since 2003 to keep the average 12-month percent change in CPI inflation within 1½ percentage points of an official target of 2½%. For the most part, inflation has been poorly anchored under IT, as both realised and expected inflation have generally fluctuated at levels above the tolerance band (Figure 1.13). This suggests that the target has lacked credibility, in part because this commitment can conflict with other policy objectives such as financial stability and full employment.

That said, a micro-currency like the króna will be difficult to manage with unconstrained capital flows, regardless of the policy framework. Liberalised capital flows undermine the ability of policymakers to achieve both macroeconomic stability and exchange rate stability, and the trade-offs implied by choosing between these two objectives appear to be intensifying as capital mobility increases (Obstfeld, 2015). Some evidence suggests that flexible exchange rates may no longer ensure monetary autonomy when capital flows are unconstrained (Rey, 2013). These limitations are magnified in Iceland relative to other countries given its small size, limited production base, and strong degree of exchange-rate pass-through, likely implying greater volatility in economic activity, inflation, or both (Central Bank of Iceland, 2010).

These considerations suggest a number of principles that can inform the monetary policy framework after the lifting of capital controls. First, policy needs to be guided by transparent objectives that are mindful of the limitations imposed by national circumstances and available policy instruments. For a target to be credible, policymakers must not only be able to achieve the target but live with the trade-offs they would imply (Frankel, 2014). Second, authorities can enhance credibility by affirming central bank independence in the face of political pressures, with well-designed complementary

Figure 1.13. **Inflation targeting does not appear to have anchored expectations**

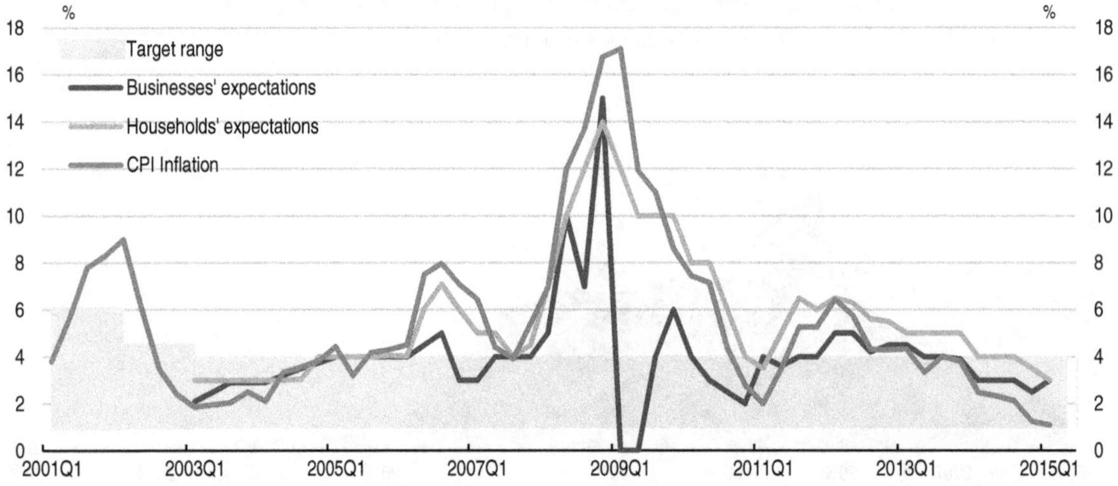

Source: Central Bank of Iceland.

StatLink http://dx.doi.org/10.1787/888933258680

measures to ensure accountability and transparency. A host of empirical research suggests that credibility, once earned, helps diminish the degree of exchange-rate pass-through to inflation (Mishkin, 2008). Third, policymakers should have an array of tools at their disposal—such as quantitative easing, interest on reserves, and so forth—that can complement or substitute for more-traditional instruments when the need arises. Credibility can enhance this toolkit by strengthening instruments that work through expectations. Fourth, mechanisms to promote fiscal policy predictability would enhance monetary policy effectiveness, albeit with sufficient flexibility to support monetary policy at times when transmission channels lack traction. Finally, to help resolve tensions that arise between inflation stability and financial stability, monetary policy should be coupled with a well-devised macroprudential framework equipped with appropriate tools to address financial imbalances and destabilising capital flows.

Fine-tuning the inflation-targeting framework

Evidence suggests that Iceland's mixed monetary policy outcomes do not derive solely from its monetary policy framework. Cross-country studies generally show that inflation targeting has been associated with improved stability of inflation and real activity, with little evidence of detrimental effects on economic growth (for example, see Pétursson, 2004). Countries with inflation targeting regimes tended to fare better than other countries during the crisis (Ólafsson and Pétursson, 2010). With regard to Iceland, previous *Economic Surveys* and the CBI itself (2012) have acknowledged that execution was partly to blame for high inflation, as policy rates were held too low for too long.

Although inflation has drifted down since the crisis to levels in line with the CBI's target, there are signs that policy still lacks credibility and that inflation expectations remain poorly anchored. The decline in inflation has been aided, in part, by the disinflationary global environment and by diminished variability in the exchange rate from capital controls. Measures of longer term expectations, such as market measures of breakeven inflation expectations five to ten years ahead (Figure 1.15), show that bond market participants still consistently expect inflation to settle above the target after short run disinflationary pressures play out. Indeed, long-run inflation expectations have surged as recent nominal wage settlements have significantly exceeded levels consistent with productivity growth and target inflation. Policymakers have thus far reacted appropriately to these developments by boosting interest rates and signalling further tightening, but credibility will be undermined if these intentions are not fulfilled.

For these reasons, it seems sensible for monetary policy to implement an inflation targeting framework following the lifting of controls that is squarely focused on the inflation target. To promote this discipline, policymakers should refrain from using policy rates for secondary objectives (such as financial stability and stabilising the exchange rate) unless better-suited tools lack traction. An aggressive tightening to forestall inflationary pressures from recent wage settlements is needed to lock in low inflation expectations and enhance credibility. The central bank should also downplay rate-setting techniques that rely upon unobservable supply variables (such as potential output and the NAIRU) that become more prominent when both full employment and low inflation are weighted by policy (Hall, 2005). Real-time estimates of economic slack can be especially misleading in Iceland (Figure 1.14). The government should be careful that proposed legislative changes, including the idea of expanding the number of governors from one to three, are not perceived to undermine the commitment to central bank independence and accountability codified into existing law. In particular, the monetary policy committee established by 2009 legislation is consistent with international best practises and should be retained.

Figure 1.14. **Real-time estimates of the Icelandic output gap can be misleading**

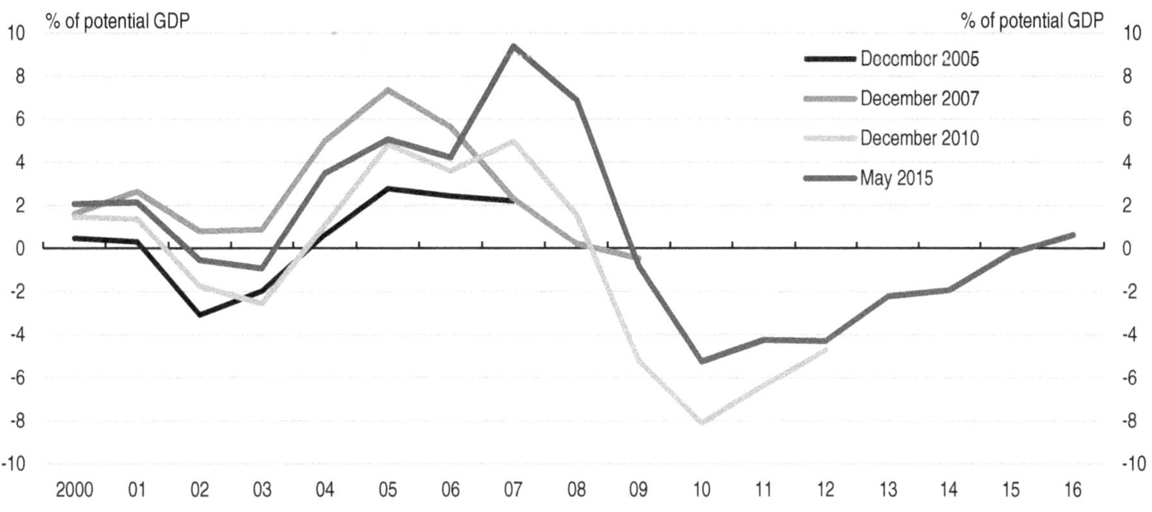

Source: OECD Economic Outlook database.

StatLink http://dx.doi.org/10.1787/888933258695

Leading into the crisis, foreign reserves were insufficient to counter the net exposure of private balance sheets to the falling króna, which came to a head when the global liquidity crunch eliminated access to foreign funding. These deficiencies contributed to the perception of a one-way bet against the króna, thereby encouraging destabilising capital flows. This experience is consistent with Catão and Milesi-Ferretti (2014), who provide evidence that the ratio of net foreign liabilities to GDP is a significant predictor of a country entering a financial crisis. Although financial stability policy could help prevent future crises, foreign exchange exposures can slip through regulatory cracks, and evidence shows

Figure 1.15. **Breakeven inflation measures suggest that expectations are not firmly anchored**

Note: Breakeven inflation expectations are calculated from yield spreads between nominal and index-linked Government and Government-backed bonds (5-day moving averages). Daily data.
Source: Central Bank of Iceland, Economic Indicators.

StatLink http://dx.doi.org/10.1787/888933258704

that currency reserves are an effective hedge against these exposures precipitating a crisis. Foreign currency reserves can also reinforce confidence as Iceland lifts its capital controls. A sizeable buffer already is in place, as the CBI has bolstered its reserves to an equivalent of nearly one-third of annual GDP (Figure 1.16), exceeding common adequacy benchmarks such as the requirement that reserves exceed the aggregate quantity of short-term foreign debt (the *Greenspan-Guidotti Rule*). Moreover, this measure likely understates reserve adequacy because aggregate short-term debt includes offshore króna claims that will have limited mobility under the plan to lift capital controls.

Figure 1.16. **Official reserves have been bolstered**

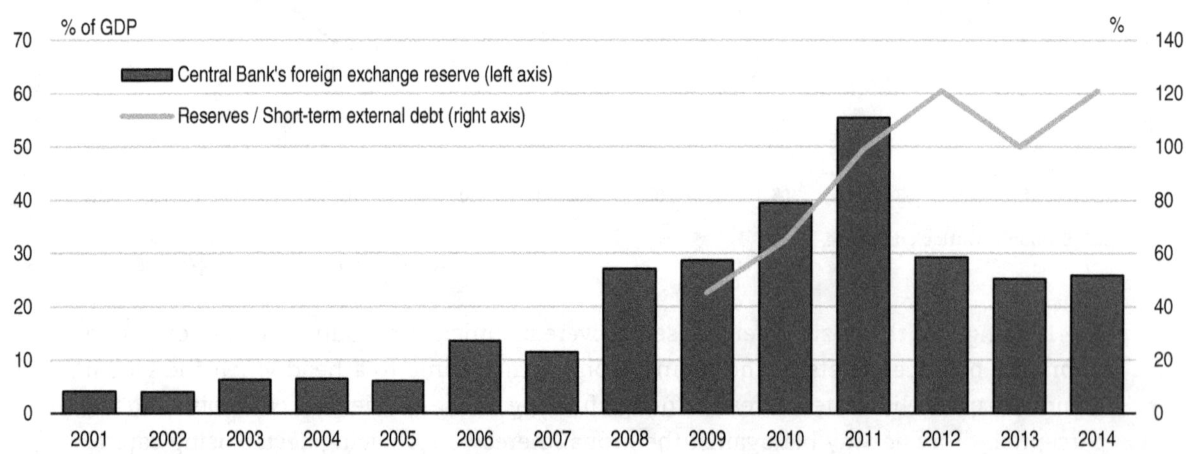

Note: Reserves and short-term debt exclude old bank related stocks.
Source: Central Bank of Iceland and IMF Country Report (Iceland) N.15/72 and N.12/309.

StatLink http://dx.doi.org/10.1787/888933258710

Monetary policy implementation might also be made easier if refinements were made to enhance the credibility of the CBI's commitment to achieve its inflation target. One possibility is to extend the target horizon to two years and to craft policy communication to focus attention away from transitory inflationary disturbances, which would help stake the central bank's credibility on containing persistent inflationary pressures rather than on its ability to smooth through transitory inflation shocks. Among other things, this would direct attention away from the effects of exogenous exchange rate shocks. Given the bluntness of monetary instruments and lags in policy implementation, attempts to smooth pass-through effects likely generate instability.

The CBI has proposed a refinement dubbed 'IT-plus' (CBI, 2010) in which inflation targeting would be complemented with small-scale, sterilised foreign currency interventions intended to smooth through excessive exchange rate fluctuations from short-term capital flows. The hope is that damping these fluctuations would forestall some of the volatility in realised and expected inflation. Although this premise is sound, the extent that limited interventions will be able to successfully lean against erratic fluctuations once controls are lifted is unclear, as such interventions could easily be swamped by international capital flows. International evidence suggests that sterilised interventions are ineffective unless backed by a credible expectation that supportive changes will be made to other instruments—such as policy rates—if necessary (Ghosh, 2008). To avoid exposing taxpayers to significant losses, the CBI will need to ensure that such interventions are perceived as credible in light of their overall policy objectives.

Building a prudential framework to support macroeconomic stability

Financial stabilisation policy holds particular promise for Iceland. Given the country's small size, incomplete international risk-sharing, and susceptibility to destabilising international capital flows, financial institutions are likely exposed to more systemic risk than in other countries. Macroprudential policy could diminish this vulnerability by forestalling the accumulation of financial system imbalances, leaning against destabilising capital flows, or both. Active policy along these lines may prove helpful for managing such vulnerabilities both during the transition from capital controls and over the longer term.

Even so, the range of potential measures to promote financial stability will be limited by Iceland's international obligations regarding capital flows, including the OECD Codes of Liberalisation of Capital Movements. Beyond these limitations, monitoring the increasingly complex financial sector will remain challenging, especially with limited resources. Experience has shown that more-stringent regulations create incentives for financial innovations to work around regulatory rules, or worse, channel activity outside of regulatory scope. The Tier 1 capital ratio—a basic benchmark of financial solvency in the Basel Accords—appears to have no value in predicting bank failures during the financial crisis, in part because banks were able to boost risk in unintended ways that were within the rules (Haldane, 2012). Such problems will be nearly impossible to overcome, which suggests that prudential policy should be backstopped with precautionary buffers that bolster resilience more broadly.

Authorities have made progress in strengthening the financial stability framework

The Icelandic authorities are making progress in overhauling the financial regulation framework to address shortcomings exposed in the lead-up to the crisis. One such shortcoming was a lack of macroprudential supervision, as financial regulation was housed in a number of bodies that had little collaboration (Althingi, 2012b). The government has codified an over-arching framework for financial stability that outlines formal responsibilities and lines of collaboration. Legislation in 2014 created a Financial Stability Council (FSC)—composed of the heads of the CBI, Financial Supervision Authority (FME), and the Ministry of Finance and Economic Affairs—with a broad mandate to formulate financial stability policy, assess threats to stability, and recommend policy actions. The FSC has been active since the fall of 2014, and is supported by a Systemic Risk Committee consisting of the heads and deputy heads of the CBI and the FME, as well as a government appointee. Ongoing co-operation and information sharing between the CBI and FME is also being codified. In this financial stability framework, the FSC formulates macroprudential policy recommendations that are then implemented by the FME and the CBI (Figure 1.17).

Figure 1.17. **Iceland's financial stability framework**

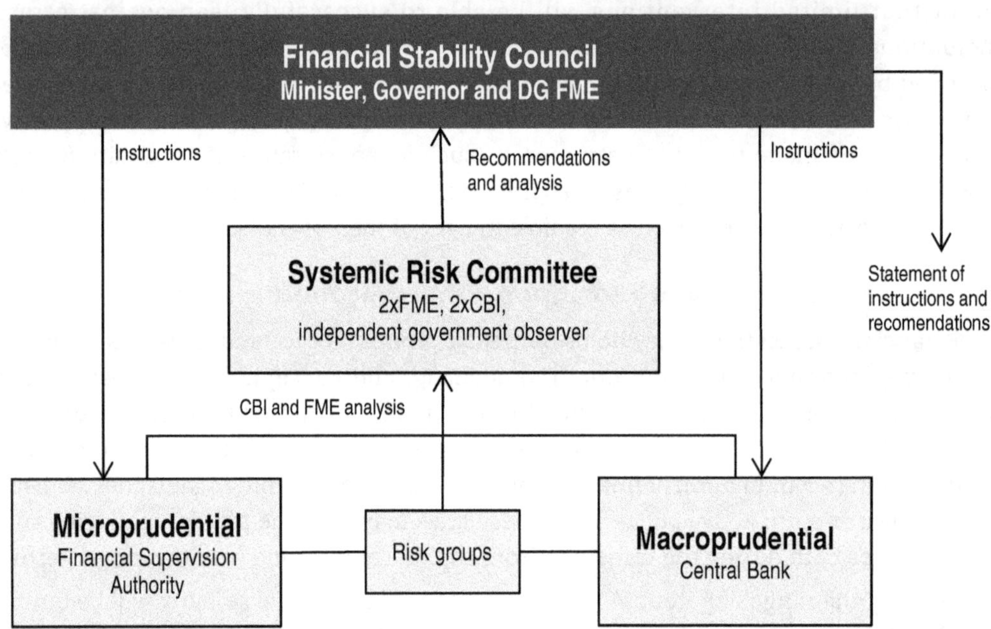

Source: Central Bank of Iceland

Integrating the various prudential regulation functions into a single independent agency might further strengthen policy by improving information sharing and minimising duplication across agencies. An integrated setup could also help mitigate conflicts of interest that might arise with monetary and macroprudential policy both housed within the CBI, as macroeconomic and financial stability objectives may not be consistent (Cecchetti and Li, 2008; Ueda and Valencia, 2014).

Significant progress has been made to re-orient the domestic financial system toward a more resilient capital structure. Like many financial institutions, Icelandic banks were highly leveraged and relied excessively on wholesale funding prior to the crisis. For now this reliance on wholesale markets has faded, as savings trapped in the country by capital controls provide an ample supply of deposits for short-term funding. Empowered by emergency statutory authority gained at the time of the crisis, the FME imposed stricter capital standards on the new banks, doubling the required capital adequacy ratios (CAR) from the Basel II minimum of 8% to 16% (FME, 2009) and has encouraged banks to maintain ample capital holdings during the process of aligning Icelandic legislation with the new Basel III standards. Rules regarding liquidity, which are implemented by the CBI, have recently been tightened as well. Partly by consequence, CARs of the three banks (Figure 1.18, Panel A) are now hovering at levels in the vicinity of 25%, and Tier 1 CARs are well in excess of the current Basel III minimum of 4%. While this more stable funding structure could raise bank intermediation costs, spreads between prime lending rates and treasuries at comparable maturities are substantially below precrisis levels (Panel B), suggesting that a less aggressive capital structure has had little influence on domestic lending rates.

Figure 1.18. **Higher capital adequacy requirements have had little influence on bank lending rates**

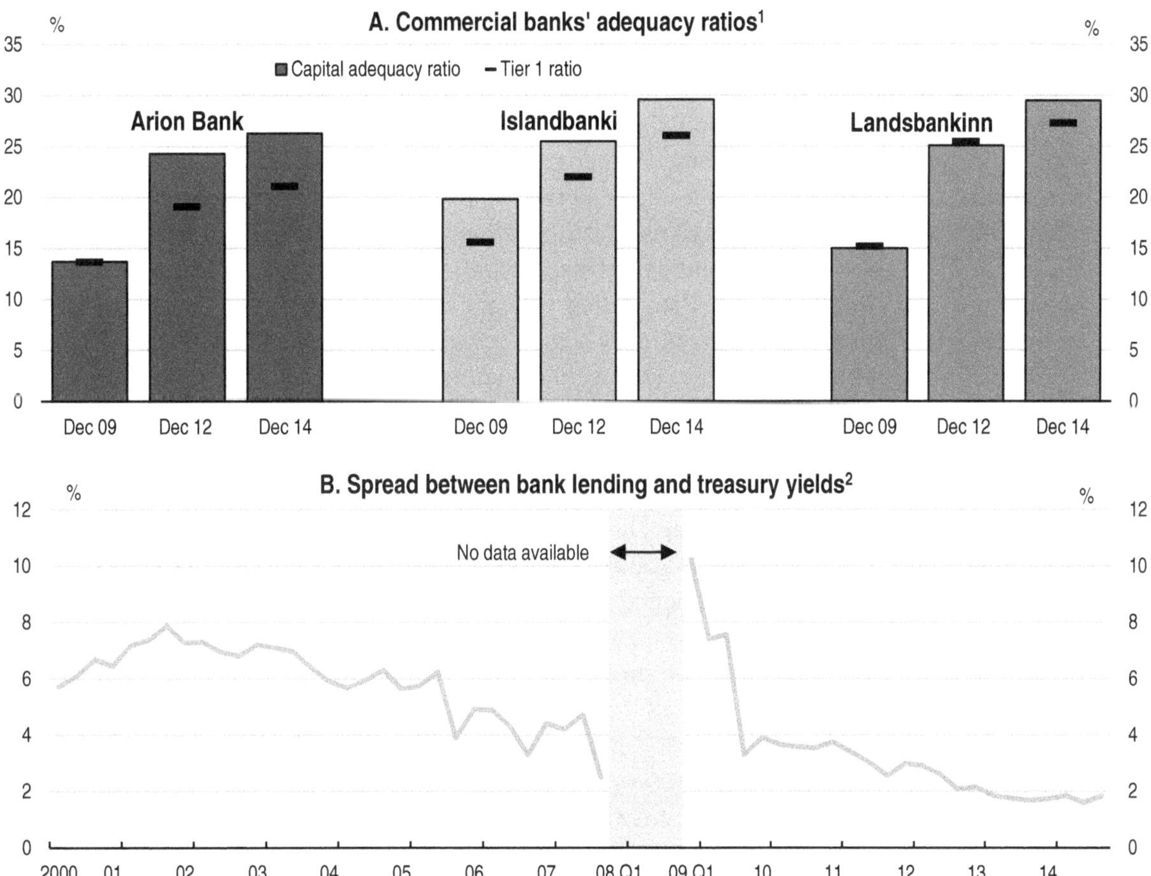

1. Consolidated accounts. The Capital Adequacy Ratio is calculated by dividing a bank's core capital by its risk-weighted asset base, while the Tier 1 ratio divides Tier 1 capital by the same base. Core capital is the sum of Tier 1 and Tier 2 capital.
2. Spread between the weighted average of interest rate on general purpose loans and the yields on 90-day treasury bills.

Sources: Commercial banks' annual and interim financial statements, Datastream.

StatLink http://dx.doi.org/10.1787/888933258722

Two of the main causes of the Icelandic bank implosion were foreign funding risk and the absence of a credible lender of last resort in foreign currency (Buiter and Sibert, 2008). Although the banks had foreign currency-denominated assets and liabilities in offsetting magnitudes, the funding was largely sourced from short-term foreign currency loans and deposits that were vulnerable to a credit crunch. With foreign currency liabilities at the banks amounting to many multiples of domestic GDP, the CBI was unable to compensate for the withdrawal of this funding. The CBI implemented new Basel III liquidity rules in 2013 designed to prevent such a situation from reoccurring. Among these rules is a liquidity coverage ratio requirement that obliges banks to hold liquid foreign currency-denominated assets in excess of specified ratios of foreign currency-denominated deposits. In 2014, the CBI also implemented *net stable funding rules* that limit maturity mismatches between banks' foreign assets and liabilities. Proposed legislation will also put limits on unhedged foreign currency borrowing. The CBI is also considering rules designed to ensure that financial institutions are able to withstand a lack of access to foreign capital markets for up to three years, and have unveiled a stress testing model to assess the vulnerability of the financial system to various shocks (CBI, 2014b).

Additional steps to strengthen the prudential environment

Work still needs to be done to address institutional deficiencies. A recent IMF Report (2014) identified numerous shortcomings regarding the FME, which has been making comprehensive reforms to address vulnerabilities revealed by the crisis. While much has been achieved, reforms have been delayed by staffing limitations (half of the authority's employees have less than five years of experience and very few have more than ten) and other pressures. In particular, prudential supervision can be less nimble in Iceland than in other countries because of restrictions that regulations and guidelines have a firm legal footing, and because of enforcement delays stemming from regulatory complexities. A lack of updated guidelines and rules regarding risk management practises of financial institutions has undermined transparency and is contributing to regulatory uncertainty. Although resources being directed to FME will help address these shortcomings over time, ongoing attention is advised to ensure that funding remains adequate and that experienced staff are retained.

The government is actively working on legislation to replace temporary prudential rules with laws that comply with the European Capital Requirements Directive (CRD IV). The directives work in upgraded Basel III standards designed to address many policy priorities, including enhanced resilience to systemic risks. Recent legislation introduced Basel III's more stringent and flexible capital adequacy requirements as well as provisions regarding employee bonuses at financial institutions, and new bills are in train to implement remaining directives. In addition to boosting the stringency of various capital adequacy and liquidity rules, CRD IV includes many new guidelines and provisions regarding financial leverage and internal governance. This expanded set of prudential tools will upgrade the financial stability framework, allowing flexibility for policymakers to tailor polices to specific vulnerabilities. Among other things, these tools will allow policymakers to counter the formation of bubbles and to adjust capital buffers to reflect counter-cyclical considerations and gradations in systemic risk across institutions and in time. In addition to transposing remaining CRD IV directives into Icelandic law, the authorities should endeavour to keep pace with the evolution of prudential tools and best practises internationally.

The authorities need to codify permanent statutory authority to deal with the problem of resolving failed financial institutions as recommended in the last *Economic Survey*. Iceland entered the crisis with no resolution authority to oversee the orderly liquidation of a failed institution. Having an authority in place can mitigate moral hazard problems, and makes it more likely that a distressed institution can be unwound using a minimum of public resources and without triggering a systemic crisis. Emergency legislation enacted during the crisis provides the FME with interim powers to resolve failing institutions. Authorities are planning legislation that would establish a permanent resolution authority that would have powers consistent with the latest EU directives (Ministry of Finance and Economic Affairs, 2014b), including strengthened restructuring tools, requirements that institutions regularly submit "living wills", and bank levies to fund the new authority.

Finally, steps are needed to normalise the financial safety net, which was expanded to a blanket guarantee of retail deposits in order to inhibit a bank run when the new banks were created. With the funding of the new banks long since stabilised, this scheme is no longer appropriate. To avoid moral hazard problems and other distortions, the blanket guarantee should be replaced by an unsubsidised system with limited coverage. It should also have a well-articulated strategy to hedge the exposure of the fund to exchange rate risk from foreign-currency denominated deposits. Given Iceland's membership in the EEA, the system would need to conform with regulations that limit coverage to an equivalent of €100 000.

Macroprudential policy tools and implementation

Although macroprudential regulation is in its infancy, countries have been experimenting with different tools. Tools aimed at damping credit cycles include caps on the loan-to-value ratio (LTV) or debt-to-income ratio (DTI), minimum capital buffers, as well as ceilings on financial leverage or credit growth. A long list of countries, including Canada, Chile, Ireland, Malaysia, New Zealand, and Norway, have implemented or are implementing credit-based rules to address systemic risks. For instance, Canada has sought to mitigate banking exposures to the housing market by imposing minimum down payment requirements, lowering the allowable LTV ratio for a refinancing, and reducing the maximum allowable mortgage amortisation term (*Economic Survey of Canada*, 2012). Some countries have been experimenting with adjusting rules to reflect risk conditions. New Zealand is working to link capital adequacy requirements for mortgages to their LTV ratios, which would automatically require financial institutions to adjust capital holdings to reflect the risks of growing leverage during a mortgage credit boom. Spain has developed formula-based loan-loss provisioning requirements that are designed to tighten lending conditions automatically as credit growth strengthens. Icelandic authorities are planning to propose legislation this fall that would enable regulators to adjust LTV caps, a tool that could prove timely if house prices continue their recent rapid ascent (Figure 1.19).

Other prudential instruments can be tailored to manage disruptive capital flows. A number of countries have experimented with unremunerated reserve requirements on foreign borrowing that are refundable after a specified period, including Chile, Columbia, and Thailand. Countries have levied taxes on certain types of capital flows (Brazil), placed restrictions on various types of currency derivative positions (Columbia and Thailand), or limits on asymmetric open positions to discourage foreign borrowing (Thailand).

Even though there is still little evidence to gauge the effectiveness of macroprudential policy, preliminary signs are encouraging. Fátas *et al.* (2009) illustrate that macro-prudential policy can pre-empt credit bubbles more effectively than raising policy rates, while Lim *et al.* (2011) show that tools targeted to prevent an overheating of the credit market (such as LTV ratio caps) significantly reduce the correlation between credit growth and GDP growth. Among the advantages of using macroprudential measures is that they can be tailored to specific risks rather than using blunter instruments that reduce overall

Figure 1.19. **House prices are accelerating relative to valuation benchmarks**

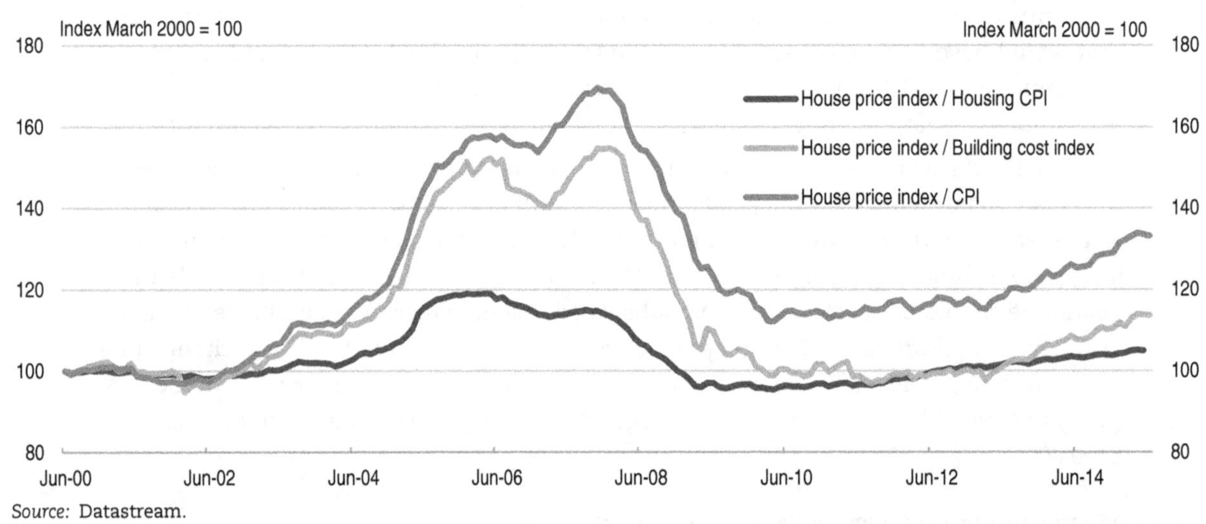

Source: Datastream.

StatLink http://dx.doi.org/10.1787/888933258735

economic activity (IMF, 2011). As for capital flow management, evidence suggests that these tools can produce favourable shifts in the composition of capital flows, such as reducing foreign exchange imbalances (Ostry *et al.*, 2012) and shifting inflows toward longer maturities (De Gregorio *et al.*, 2000).

On the other hand, there are potential disadvantages to manipulating these macroprudential levers. In contrast with the Icelandic experience to date, in other countries financial institutions tend to pass on more restrictive capital requirements in the form of somewhat higher lending rates (Basel Committee on Banking Supervision, 2010; Hanson *et al.*, 2010). It is also possible that policies which work well in some settings may not transfer to others. The history of financial regulation is also replete with instances where measures of financial risk became ineffective after they become the target of policy (Goodhart, 1981), in part because financial institutions can circumvent rules. This consideration could argue for tackling macroprudential supervision with a diverse set of instruments, combined with precautionary buffers as a last line of defense.

The authorities should also be mindful that manipulating regulatory instruments could backfire by sending negative signals about the soundness of the financial system (Eichengreen and Rose, 2014). Among other things, the possibility of adverse signalling suggests that adjustments to macroprudential policy instruments should be considered regularly within a transparent framework rather than being *ad hoc*.

Fiscal policy

With gross government debt exploding to levels approaching 100% of GDP in the wake of the financial crisis, Iceland designed a fiscal consolidation programme to place public finances on a sounder footing, restore access to outside lending, reduce the sovereign risk premium, and reduce vulnerability to future crises. Consolidation to date has been substantial. The projected primary surplus for 2015 (excluding one-offs) is about 10% of GDP higher than in 2009 (Figure 1.21), gross debt has fallen by nearly 20% of GDP, and the sovereign risk premium now stands at just a fraction of its crisis high (Figure 1.20).

Figure 1.20. **Spreads for Icelandic treasuries have narrowed**

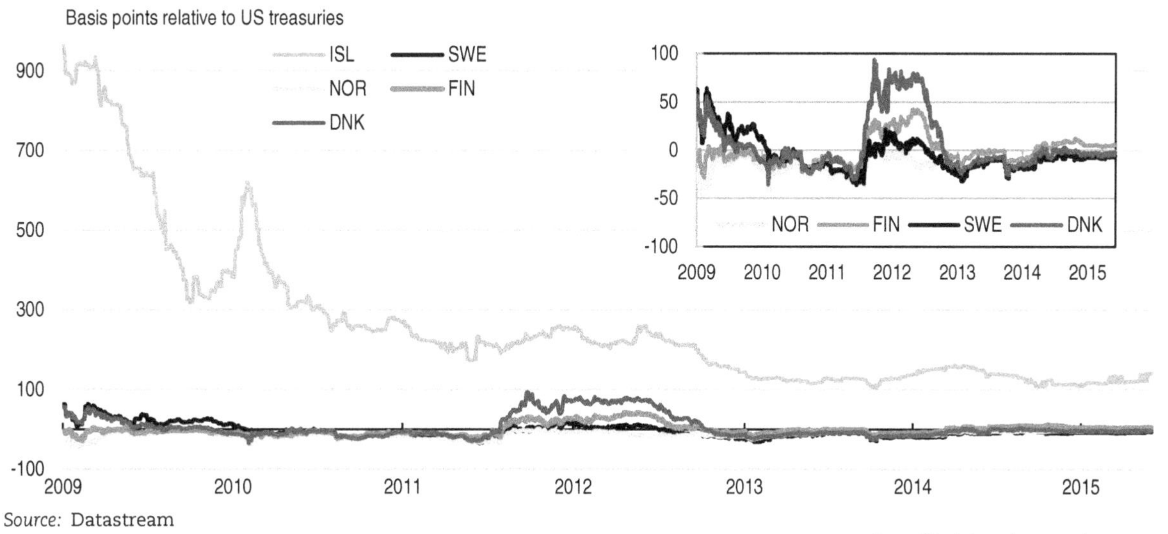

Source: Datastream

StatLink http://dx.doi.org/10.1787/888933258742

Assuming that upcoming budget surpluses average about 0.5% of GDP as projected and that economic activity increases in line with expectations, the debt-to-GDP ratio should fall below the target of 60% (by the national accounts definition, which excludes estimated liabilities for underfunding of government-employee pension schemes) by 2019.

Although high relative to GDP, Iceland's gross debt burden is more sustainable than initial appearances suggest. The liability for the public employee pension scheme, which is typically not included in the estimates for countries with pay-as-you-go schemes, boosts gross debt by roughly 20 percentage points relative to GDP, but will not increase over time because future obligations are now being set aside in a fully funded scheme. Much of the debt is also offset by financial assets, which are valued at nearly 60% of GDP. These assets include foreign exchange funds deposited in the CBI to bolster official foreign reserves (about 25% of GDP), and equity in the new Landsbanki valued at nearly 20% of GDP. The plan to unwind the failed bank estates is also expected to yield one-off revenues between 18% and 42% of GDP to the treasury. The government intends to repay some debt using these one-off revenues, along with the proceeds from selling 30% of their Landsbankinn stake. The CBI has also been gradually accumulating foreign exchange reserves through official interventions, which will allow the government to pare its borrowed reserves. Debt is also structured in a way that should help minimise risk exposures (IMF, 2015b), as the vast bulk of instruments pay fixed interest rates, are denominated in króna, and are held domestically.

Future consolidation is subject to risks that highlight the need for fiscal discipline. Although the projected debt servicing profile seems manageable, there are pressure points ahead when relatively large bond holdings come due, including some that are foreign denominated. Official debt totals also exclude contingent government liabilities arising from debt guarantees for state-owned enterprises that back principal amounting to 59% of GDP. These guarantees are linked to just two entities, the Housing Finance Fund (HFF) and the National Power Company, thereby exposing government finances to mortgage credit risk and fluctuations in prices of energy-intensive export goods.

Figure 1.21. **Public finances are recovering from the crisis**

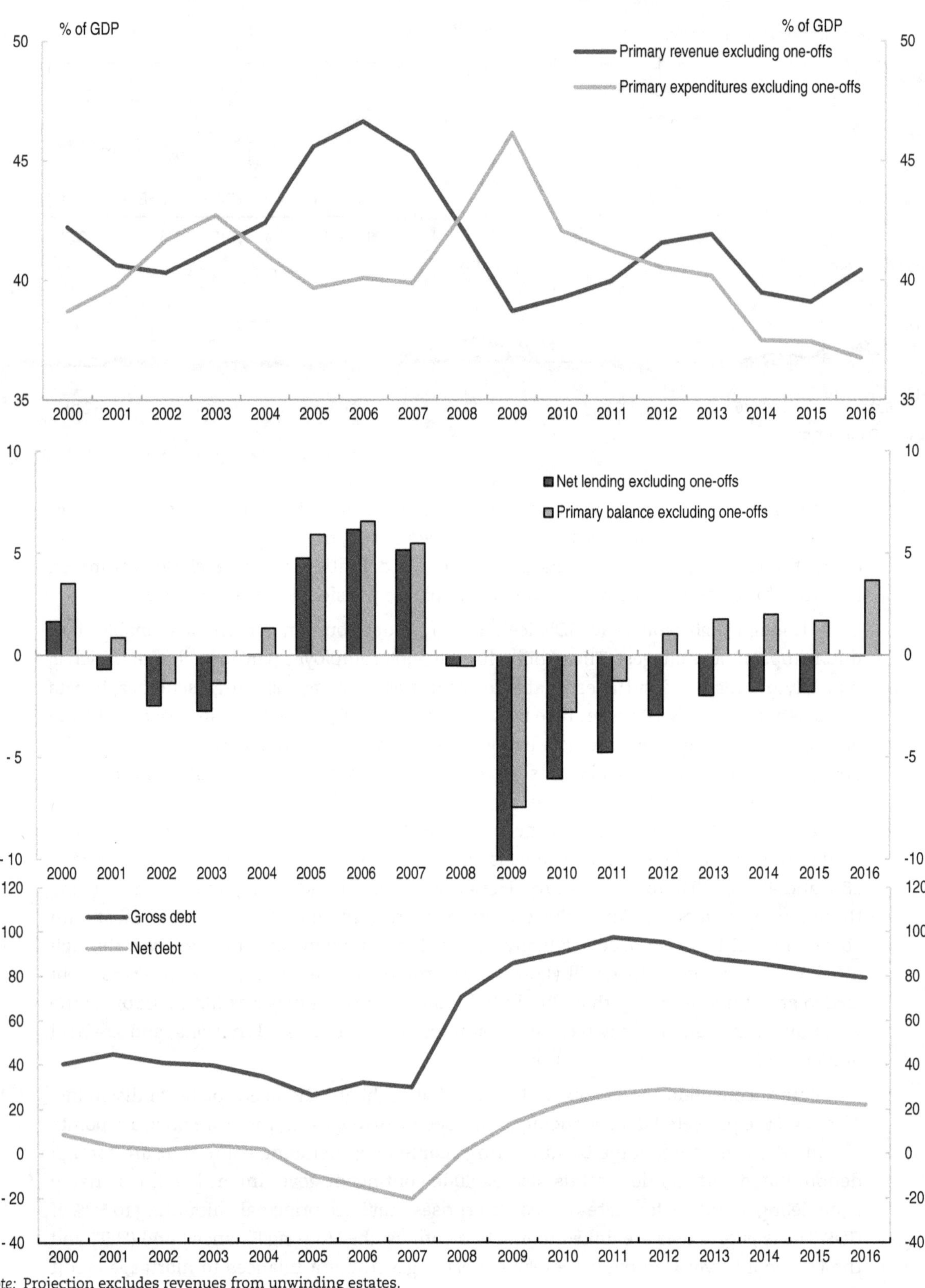

Note: Projection excludes revenues from unwinding estates.

Source: OECD National Accounts database; one-offs are IMF estimates.

StatLink http://dx.doi.org/10.1787/888933258759

These contingent liabilities have fallen by about 20% of GDP since the crisis because the HFF portfolio has shrunk, as the authorities have ceased its current lending operations and are allowing mortgage finance activity to migrate to the banking sector. The dormancy of the HFF—which had long been the dominant player in the residential mortgage market—is a welcome development, as the fund's implicit subsidy had been the source of a number of distortions. As discussed in OECD (2008), the HFF's funding advantage allowed it to offer mortgage lending terms that often seemed immune to monetary conditions, thereby weakening monetary policy transmission and pushing households into owner-occupancy rather than renting. This subsidy backfired following the crisis, as the fund's substantial losses required a government recapitalisation. HFF capitalisation remains very low. The HFF should be wound down, as social housing objectives can be satisfied more efficiently by resources (recently allocated to facilitate the wage settlement process) to fund supply and demand incentives for the rental market specifically targeted to low-income housing.

The bulk of Iceland's sovereign debt can be traced to the government's role in backstopping the economy during and after the crisis. Even though a government bailout of the failed banks was impossible, the expenses needed to carve out the domestic assets of the failed bank estates, re-capitalise the financial system, and to fulfil asset guarantees (such as domestic deposit insurance) still required immense public outlays. According to Laeven and Valencia (2012), direct restructuring outlays amounted to about 45% of Icelandic GDP. The total legacy of the crisis on gross government debt, after adding in the fallout from the crisis on the deficit and government borrowing to reinforce foreign exchange reserves, likely approaches the total increase in gross debt since 2007, or about two-thirds of GDP (see Einarsson *et al.*, 2015). Some of this debt may be temporary, as it helped fund financial assets that can be sold. Nevertheless, this illustrates the potential scale of public liquidity that may be called upon in a severe crisis scenario, even if the government's role is limited to restructuring the banking system.

A fiscal framework is needed to lock in budgetary discipline

With public finances on the mend, the government should establish a framework to guide long-term fiscal policy. Given ongoing economic vulnerabilities, it seems appropriate to adopt a precautionary approach designed to limit public debt so that public resources can be deployed in the event of a future financial crisis (Obstfeld, 2013; Ostry *et al.*, 2010). Furthermore, maintaining fiscal space can help fortify the financial sector by raising confidence that the government will be able to contain the economic fallout from a future crisis. Limiting debt over the long haul will require disciplined budgeting, which may be difficult to sustain in the face of short-term political pressures. Codifying this discipline into law would guard against such pressure.

Beyond buffering against a financial collapse, a precautionary fiscal approach preserves the option of applying stimulus in the event of a future financial crisis. As economic downturns associated with financial crises tend to be deeper and more prolonged (Reinhart and Rogoff, 2009), fiscal policy may need to supplement monetary policy to stabilise aggregate demand. This is especially true if monetary policy transmission channels become clogged, as they did in many OECD countries following the crisis when policy rates hit the zero lower bound. This potential benefit is consistent with evidence that countries entering financial crises with more government debt tend to have deeper and more prolonged downturns.

Beyond maintaining the capacity for fiscal policy to assist monetary policy following deep recessions, there is also a need to codify principles that improve policy co-ordination more broadly. Numerous studies, such as the CBI (2012) and the IMF (2012b), have highlighted episodes where Iceland's fiscal policy stance unexpectedly pulled against monetary policy. This lack of coordination is rooted in various shortcomings of the existing fiscal framework that undermine discipline (IMF, 2012c):

- A lack of principles and procedures for macroeconomic forecasting and fiscal policymaking;
- A budget formulation process that is fragmented (parliamentary discussions are focused on 260 separate agencies rather than on their parent ministries) and relatively unconstrained;
- Loopholes in budget execution that allow the government to overspend its budget with impunity;
- No integration with local levels of government; and
- Little emphasis on providing comprehensive and timely data to inform fiscal decisions.

Given monetary policy transmission lags, guidelines that encourage a more predictable impetus from fiscal policy to aggregate demand would support macroeconomic stabilisation.

The proposed Organic Budget Law seemingly addresses most of these basic requirements (see Box 1.2), outlining a disciplined framework that will anchor annual budgets on medium-term objectives designed to reduce total government debt. The proposal specifies a 30% long-run target for a specific net debt-to-GDP ratio (a measure that excludes unfunded public pension liabilities and other accounts payable from gross debt, and currency and deposits from financial assets; by this measure, net debt in 2014 would have amounted to about 55% of GDP). Under normal conditions, annual overall deficits would be capped at 2.5% of GDP, while net lending would need to be positive over five-year periods. When the debt-to-GDP ratio exceeds the 30% target, subsequent budgets would need to reduce the excess by at least 5 percent annually, on average, over the following three years. The proposal also builds in flexibility to suspend these constraints if specified conditions are met, which should mitigate the risk that policy will become pro-cyclical in a downturn. In such circumstances, the fiscal policy stance can temporarily move to stimulus.

Consistent with the need for policy coordination, the law aims to make fiscal policy more predictable and less susceptible to adjustments during the budget year. An independent fiscal oversight council would be created to assess the budget's adherence to the fiscal rules and medium-term objective, and that could also evaluate longer-term threats to fiscal policy. Provisions of the proposed law include a budget contingency reserve, and some care will be required to ensure that this reserve is used as a safety valve rather than to accommodate slippage in budget implementation. Although the fiscal council can help monitor these contingencies, amendments to the law may become necessary if this reserve is abused.

The discipline imposed by the law would play an important role in replenishing fiscal space that evaporated during the crisis. Figure 1.22 shows simulated budget outcomes under various assumptions regarding the government's budgetary balances and usage of one-off revenues. The projections evaluate the paths of gross debt (the government uses a

Box 1.2. Main provisions of the Organic Budget Law

Fiscal Rules

- The annual deficit cannot exceed 2.5% of GDP and net lending must be positive over five-year periods.
- The net debt-to-GDP ratio should remain below a long-run target of 30% of GDP (debt excludes unfunded public pension liabilities and other accounts payable; financial assets exclude currency and deposits). If the ratio exceeds this target, 5% of the excess must be worked down annually, on average, over every three year period.
- The preceding rules may be suspended for up to two years in the event of an economic downturn or other event that materially undermines the stated economic assumptions underlying the budget.

Overall budget transparency and accountability

- When starting a new term, the government must present a *Fiscal Policy Statement* outlining its objectives. These objectives abide by legally binding principles of *stability*, *sustainability*, *predictability*, *prudence*, and *transparency*.
- Each year the government must submit for parliamentary approval a *Medium-Term Fiscal Strategy* (MTFS) for the upcoming five-year period that sets out numerical objectives for central and local government budget balances and long-term liabilities. Agreements between levels of government about their targets must be reached in advance, thereby integrating local governments. Annual budgets must be consistent with the MTFS, with revisions permitted only under certain circumstances.
- An independent Fiscal Council of impartial appointees with relevant postgraduate training has the authority to assess whether budgets adhere to the principles and to the MTFS.
- Governments must publish audited annual financial statements structured to show compliance with its objectives and the law.

Budget formulation and approval

- Appropriations are made directly to ministries based upon policy plans for the following five years. Ministers decide on appropriations within their portfolio, with discretion to re-allocate funding within specified limits.
- A contingency reserve not to exceed 2% of total expenditure may be used under specified conditions.
- To ensure consistency with the MTFS, the Parliament's powers are limited to budgetary changes that do not increase expenditures, reduce revenue, or increase liabilities. Parliamentary debate regarding expenditures, revenues, and liabilities follows a top-down approach, starting with the overall budget and then sequentially stepping down through the ministerial and programme/policy area levels.

Budget execution

- Within each ministry, overspending from previous years cannot be carried over, while underspending can be carried over within specified limits, for certain types of spending.
- Parliament must authorize unbudgeted expenditures that cannot be funded by reallocating resources within a ministry or from the contingency reserve.
- Audits will be conducted to report overspending or financial irregularities to Parliament, which may then investigate and assess penalties.

Figure 1.22. **Simulations of public debt paths**

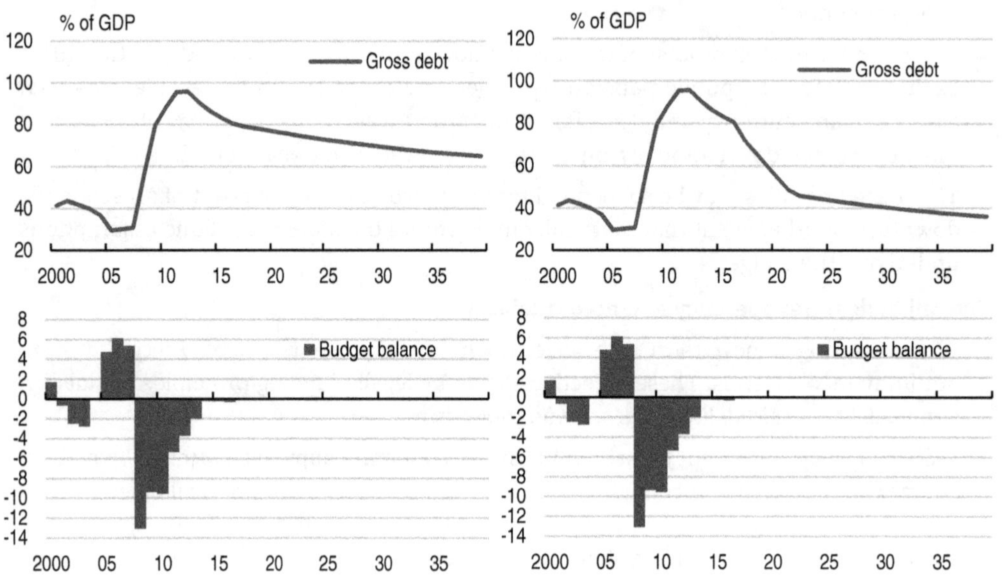

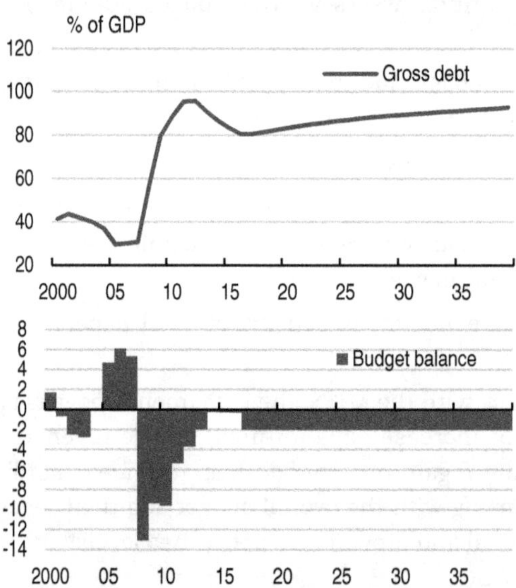

Note: Simulations follow the OECD projection through 2016. Thereafter, real GDP growth averages 2.4% and inflation averages 2.5%. In simulations A and C, financial assets are kept constant at their latest projected level (57.3%).
Source: OECD Economic Outlook database and OECD calculations.

StatLink http://dx.doi.org/10.1787/888933258468

slightly different debt measure, but the implications are qualitatively identical for both measures) and are conditioned upon assumptions about potential real GDP growth, inflation, and interest rates. Keeping the budget balanced in line with the proposed law, while maintaining financial assets constant at their 2013 level relative to GDP (Panel A), would virtually eliminate the net debt excluding contingent liabilities and unfunded public pension schemes. Gross debt will decline even more rapidly if the budget is kept balanced and authorities use the stability contributions and proceeds from the sale of Landsbanki to repay debt (Panel B), to below 40% of GDP by 2040. However, if fiscal policy reverts to deficits of 2% of GDP in line with historical norms and one-off revenues are not directed to repay debt (Panel C), gross debt reverses direction and climbs to nearly 100% of GDP by 2040.

Recommendations for promoting macroeconomic stability and resiliency

Key recommendations

- Progress is needed in lifting Iceland's capital controls and the current plan is a welcome step in this direction. Maintaining a robust macroeconomic stability framework will help avoid a disorderly outcome.
- Monetary policy needs to raise interest rates to ensure that a wage-price spiral does not develop, as already stated by the Monetary Policy Committee. The focus should remain on low and stable inflation over the medium term, while allowing the exchange rate to float apart from limited interventions to smooth erratic fluctuations.
- To protect macroeconomic stability the central bank should remain independent from political interference. The monetary policy committee introduced in 2009 should be retained.
- Strengthen the macro-prudential policy framework, incorporating tools to address large swings in capital flows unrelated to fundamentals, while respecting international commitments.
- To protect the economy from unavoidable shocks and reinforce confidence, buffers should be built up including ample fiscal space, foreign exchange reserves and bank capital and liquidity.
- Pass and implement the Organic Budget Law, including enacting the balanced budget rules and establishing an independent Fiscal Council to assess progress towards sustainability.
- Use windfall gains and one-off revenues to pay down debt, including any proceeds from lifting the capital controls.
- Avoid accumulating further contingent liabilities, including by closing the Housing Financing Fund (HFF).

Other recommendations

- Consider refinements to the inflation target such as a lengthened target horizon that might enhance credibility by placing emphasis on persistent inflationary pressures that policy is well equipped to address.
- To safeguard the perceived independence of monetary policy, appointments to the committee should be for staggered fixed terms and should continue to be made on the basis of professional experience.

Bibliography

Ahrend, R., A. Goujard, and C. Schwellnus (2012), "International Capital Mobility: Which Structural Policies Reduce Financial Fragility?", *OECD Economic Policy Working Paper*, June.

Althingi (2012a), *Future Structure of the Icelandic Financial System*, Report of the Minister of Economic Affairs to the Althingi, March.

Barajas, A., G. Dell'Ariccia, and A. Levchenko (2007), "Credit Booms: the Good, the Bad, and the Ugly," IMF unpublished manuscript, Washington, DC, November.

Basel Committee on Banking Supervision (2010), "An Assessment of the Long-term Economic Impact of Stronger Capital and Liquidity Requirements", Bank for International Settlements, August.

Buiter, W., and A. Slbert (2008), "The Icelandic banking crisis and what to do about it: The lender of last resort theory of optimal currency areas," *CEPR Policy Insight Working Paper* No. 26.

Catão, L. and G. Milesi-Ferretti (2014), "External Liabilities and Crises", *Journal of International Economics* Vol. 94(1), 18-32.

Cecchetti, S. and L. Li (2008), "Do capital adequacy requirements matter for monetary policy?", *Economic Inquiry*, Vol. 46(4), 643-659.

Central Bank of Iceland (2008), "The Effect of Exchange Rate Movements on Inflation", *Central Bank of Iceland Monetary Bulletin* 2008-2, July.

Central Bank of Iceland (2010), "Monetary Policy in Iceland after Capital Controls", *Special Publication* No. 4, December.

Central Bank of Iceland (2011), "Capital Account Liberalisation Strategy", Report to the minister of economic affairs, March.

Central Bank of Iceland (2012a), "Financial Stability: The Role of the Central Bank of Iceland," A report by Sir Andrew Large at the Request of the Central Bank of Iceland," *Special Publication* No. 8, October.

Central Bank of Iceland (2012b), "Prudential Rules following Capital Controls," *Special Publication* No. 6, August.

Central Bank of Iceland (2012c), "Iceland's Currency and Exchange Rate Policy Options", *Special Publication* No. 7, September. (NB: Executive chapter summaries in English are available at *http://www.cb.is/publications-and-speeches/publications/special-publications/special-publication-7/*).

Central Bank of Iceland (2014a), "Progress of the Plan for Removal of Capital Controls", *Report of the CBI to the Althingi*, September.

Central Bank of Iceland (2014b), "Financial Stability Report", *Informational Report 2014/1*, April.

Central Bank of Iceland (2014c), "Financial Stability Report", *Informational Report* 2014/2, October.

Central Bank of Iceland (2014d), "Monetary Bulletin", *Informational Report* 2014/2, March.

Central Bank of Iceland (2015a), "Underlying international investment position at year-end 2014," *Special Publication* No. 6, March.

Central Bank of Iceland (2015b), "Financial Stability Report", *Informational Report* 2015/1, April.

De Gregorio, J., S. Edwards, and R. Valdés (2000), "Controls on Capital Inflows: Do They Work?" *Journal of Development Economics*, Vol. 63, 59–83.

Desai, M., C. Foley and J. Hines, Jr. (2005), "Foreign Direct Investment and the Domestic Capital Stock," *American Economic Review*, Vol. 95 (May), 33-38.

Eichengreen, B., and A. Rose (2014), "Capital Controls in the 21st Century", *Centre for Economic Policy Research Policy Insight* No. 72, June.

Einarsson, B. G., K. Gunnlaugsson, T. T. Ólafsson and T. G. Pétursson (2015), "The Long History of Financial Boom-Bust Cycles in Iceland – Part I: Financial Crises" *Central Bank of Iceland Working Paper*, forthcoming.

Engel, C. (2012), "Capital Controls: What Have We Learned?", *Bank for International Settlements Paper* No. 68f.

Frankel, J. (2014), "Emerging and developing countries should work on targeting NGDP", *The Guardian*, June 24.

Ghosh, A. (2008), "Turning Currencies Around", *Finance and Development*, Vol. 45(2), 41-43.

Goodhart, Charles (1981), "Problems of Monetary Management: The U.K. Experience", Anthony S. Courakis (ed.), *Inflation, Depression, and Economic Policy in the West* (Rowman & Littlefield), 111–146.

Haldane, A. (2012), "The Dog and the Frisbee", *Speech given at the Economic Policy Symposium - Jackson Hole, Federal Reserve Bank of Kansas City*, August.

Hall, R. E. (2005). "Separating the business cycle from other economic fluctuations," *Proceedings - Economic Policy Symposium - Jackson Hole, Kansas City Federal Reserve*, August, 133-179.

Hanson, S., A. Kashyap, and J. Stein (2010), "An Analysis of the Impact of Substantially Heightened Capital Requirements on Large Financial Institutions", *Working Paper University of Chicago Booth School of Business and Harvard University*.

Haskel, J., S. Pereira, and M. Slaughter (2008), "Does Inward Foreign Direct Investment Boost the Productivity of Domestic Firms?", *The Review of Economics and Statistics*, vol. 89(3), 482–496

IMF (2012a), "The Liberalization and Management of Capital Flows: An Institutional View," November.

IMF (2012b), "Iceland: Technical Assistance Report on a New Organic Budget Law", *IMF Country Report* No. 12/4, January.

IMF (2014), "Iceland: Report on Observance of Standards and Codes (ROSC)", *IMF Country Report* No. 14/257, August.

IMF (2015a), "Iceland: Selected Issues Paper", *IMF Country Report* No. 15/73, March.

IMF (2015b), "Iceland: Article IV Consultation and Fifth Post-Program Monitoring Discussions", *IMF Country Report* No. 15/72, March.

Korinek, A. (2011), "The New Economics of Prudential Capital Controls," *IMF Economic Review*, vol. 59, no. 3, pp. 523–561.

Kose, A., E. Presad, and M. Terrones (2008), "Does Openness to International Financial Flows Raise Productivity Growth?", NBER Working Paper no. 14558.

Laeven, L., and F. Valencia (2012), "Systemic Banking Crises Database: An Update," *IMF Working Paper* No. 12/163, June.

Lim, C., F. Columba, A. Costa, P. Kongsamut, A. Otani, M. Saiyid, T. Wezel, and X. Wu (2011), "Macroprudential Policy: What Instruments and How to Use Them? Lessons from Country Experiences", *IMF Working Paper* No. 238.

Ministry of Finance and Economic Affairs (2014a), "Progress of the Plan for Removal of Capital Controls", *A report as provided for in Act No. 16/2013 of the Icelandic parliament Althingi*, September.

Ministry of Finance and Economic Affairs (2014b), "Reform of Financial Market Legislation", *Report on work on financial market legislation in the 144th session of the Althingi*, September.

Mishkin, F. (2008), "Exchange Rate Pass-through and Monetary Policy", *NBER Working Paper* No. 13889.

Modigliani, F. and M. Miller (1958), "The Cost of Capital, Corporation Finance and the Theory of Investment", *American Economic Review*, Vol. 48(3), June, 261-297.

Obstfeld, M. (2013), "On Keeping Your Powder Dry: Fiscal Foundations of Financial and Price Stability", *Monetary and Economic Studies*, Vol. (31), November.

Obstfeld, M. (2015), "Trilemmas and Tradeoffs: Living with Financial Globalisation", *Bank for International Settlements Working Paper* No. 480, January.

OECD (1991), *Economic Survey of Iceland 1991*, Paris.

OECD (2008), *Economic Survey of Iceland 2008*, Paris.

OECD (2011), *OECD Code of Liberalisation of Capital Movements 2011*, Paris.

OECD (2012), *Economic Survey of Canada 2012*, Paris.

Ólafsson and Pétursson (2010), "Weathering the Financial Storm: The Importance of Fundamentals and Flexibility", In *The Euro Area and the Financial Crisis* (eds. M. Beblavý, D. Cobham and L. Ódor). Cambridge: Cambridge University Press.

Ostry, J., A. Ghosh, J. Kim, and M. Qureshi (2010), "Fiscal Space", *IMF Position Note* SPN 10/11, September.

Ostry, J., A. Ghosh, M. Chamon, and M. Qureshi (2012), "Tools for Managing Financial-Stability Risks from Capital Outflows", *Journal of International Economics*, vol. 88, 407-421.

Ostry, J., A. Ghosh, K. Habermeier, M. Chamon, M. Qureshi, and D. Reinhardt (2010), "Capital Inflows: The Role of Controls", *IMF Staff Discussion Note*, SDN/10/04.

Ostry, J., A. Ghosh, K. Habermeier, L. Laeven, M. Chamon, M. Qureshi, and A. Kokenyne (2011), "Managing Capital Inflows: What Tools to Use?", *IMF Staff Discussion Note*, SDN/11/06; 5 April.

Pétursson, T. (2004), "The Effects of Inflation Targeting on Macroeconomic Performance", *Central Bank of Iceland Working Paper*, No. 23, June.

Pétursson, T. G., (2009), "Does inflation targeting lead to excessive exchange rate volatility?", *Central Bank of Iceland Working Paper* No. 43.

Pétursson, T. G., (2010), "Inflation control around the world: Why are some countries more successful than others?" in *Twenty Years of Inflation Targeting: Lessons Learned and Future Prospects*, Eds. D. Cobham, Ø. Eitrheim, S. Gerlach and J. F. Qvigstad. Cambridge: Cambridge University Press.

Reinhart, C. M., and V. R. Reinhart (2008), "Capital Flow Bonanzas: An Encompassing View of the Past and Present," *NBER Working Paper* no. 14321, September.

Rey, H. (2013), "Dilemma not Trilemma: The Global Financial Cycle and Monetary Policy Independence", paper presented at the Jackson Hole Symposium, August.

Reinhart, C. M., and K. S. Rogoff (2009), *This Time Is Different: Eight Centuries of Financial Folly*, Princeton: Princeton University Press.

Rogoff, K. (1999), "International Institutions for Reducing Global Financial Instability," *Journal of Economic Perspectives*, vol. 13(4), 21-42.

Rose, A.K. (2010), "Exchange Rate Regimes in the Modern Era: Fixed, Floating, and Flaky" *Journal of Economic Literature*, vol. 49(3), 652-72.

Svensson, L. (2011), "Optimal monetary policy in open economies", in Benjamin M. Friedman and Michael Woodford, editors, *Handbook of Monetary Economics*, Vol. 3B, 861–933.

Ueda, K., and F. Valencia (2014), "Central Bank Independence and Macro-prudential Regulation", *Economics Letters*, Vol. 125(2), 327-330.

World Economic Forum (2015), *Global Competitiveness Report 2014-2015*, Oxford University Press.

Chapter 2

Supporting long-term growth by improving the business environment

Iceland has a high standard of living in international comparison, but amongst OECD countries its relative ranking has been sliding. In the wake of the financial crisis, investment slumped and while the economic recovery has progressed, growth is appreciably slower than during the previous expansion. In particular, labour productivity growth has remained very weak. Against this background, policies that improve the business environment will help lift productivity growth through encouraging innovation and competition. A wide range of policies can have an impact. The regulatory environment for product markets is generally among the least restrictive economies in the OECD, but the regulatory stance is uneven. Regulations governing barriers to entrepreneurship are notably more restrictive. Strengthening competitive pressure is another means of encouraging greater efficiency and innovation, but achieving this is complicated in a small economy. Raising human capital levels amongst certain groups will also boost growth and facilitating resource reallocation can play a role in reacting to economic shocks while supporting productivity growth. Finally, public policy fostering innovation and firm creation can underpin a dynamic part of the economy, which would otherwise experience financing difficulties.

Iceland has a high standard of living in international comparison, but productivity growth has been sluggish recently. As a consequence, Iceland's ranking within the OECD has slipped and now lies slightly above average for OECD countries (Figure 2.1). This decline in standing reflects the impact of the financial crisis and weak labour productivity growth, which more than offset high participation rates and long hours worked. With labour force participation already high, stronger growth will therefore require more business investment and more dynamic multifactor productivity. Multifactor productivity has been relatively resilient recently, putting the onus on capital deepening to raise labour productivity growth.

Figure 2.1. **GNI per capita is slightly above average**

2013, estimates in US dollars, current prices, current PPPs

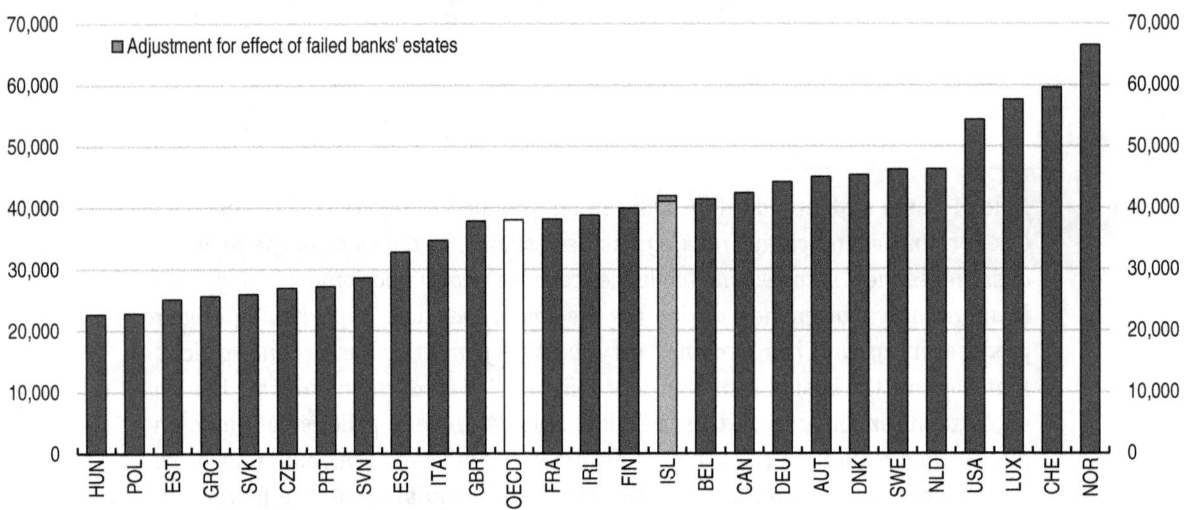

Note: OECD average excludes Mexico and Turkey.

Source: OECD, National Accounts database, Central Bank of Iceland (adjustments)

StatLink http://dx.doi.org/10.1787/888933258490

This chapter first examines the business sector in Iceland, documenting the main features. It then turns to assessing regulatory burdens. Next it discusses competition policy issues. This is followed by a consideration of labour and human capital issues and then how capital markets affect the business environment. The final section looks at support mechanisms for firm creation.

Iceland's business sector

The small size of the economy affects the business environment. Because possible exploitation of economies of scale and scope are limited, most Icelandic firms are small by international comparison. As a consequence, firms can be relatively inefficient. A second complication flowing from the small size of the country is that firm concentration within sectors can be very high, raising competition concerns. A final complication in a small country is the risk of tacit collusion and cartel behaviour.

According to official numbers there are around 66,500 firms registered in Iceland, although many are dormant. In the period since the crisis (2008-2014) 16,519 new companies were registered. Of these, 14% are in wholesale, retail or motor vehicle repairs, 13% in finance and insurance, 12% in real estate, 11% in specialist, technology and science, 6% in leasing and other specialized services and 5% in fishing and agriculture.

As in all countries, the great majority of Icelandic firms are small or medium sized (SMEs) but the Icelandic economy relies more on SMEs than EU countries in terms of employment and value added. According to the latest available comparable data (2012) and excluding firms in agriculture, forestry and fisheries, 72% of employees in Iceland work in SMEs compared to 67% in the EU. The difference in value added is even greater, with roughly 70% of value added contributed by SMEs in Iceland compared to roughly 58% in the EU-28 (SBA Factsheet Iceland 2014).

Iceland's business sector has four main sectors (McKinsey, 2012). Capital-intensive resource-based industries – fisheries and metallurgy –, combined with tourism, account for most of the export-oriented sector. A smaller international sector consists of other firms exposed to international competition, including business and ICT services, as well as some manufacturing. The remaining two sectors are the public sector and private domestic services, which together account for 70% of employment. Apart from the metallurgy sector, foreign ownership is relatively limited, partly as a result of restrictions but also due to the strong presence of state-ownership in the energy sector.

Fisheries, energy and energy-intensive industries have traditionally been the pillars of the Icelandic economy. Iceland has abundant energy resources compared to the size of the local population, and most of the energy generated (hydroelectric or geothermal) is sold to energy-intensive industries such as aluminium smelters and ferro-silicon producers. The increasing share of the energy sector in GDP is due to investment projects in energy generation from the abundant geothermal and hydroelectric resources as well as the accompanying build-up of energy-intensive industries (Table 2.1). There is still scope for further expansion, but environmental concerns play an important role in determining where and how much remaining energy sources will be harnessed. The price of energy to energy-intensive industries is strongly linked to product prices and is often denoted in foreign currency. As a result, revenues of the power companies are strongly correlated to fluctuations in the foreign exchange rate, but since the debt of the power companies is also mostly denominated in foreign currency the result is a natural hedge against currency fluctuations.

Table 2.1. **Share of different sectors in GDP**

In per cent

Industry	1997	2007	2014
Fishing	8.1	4.1	4.9
Fish processing	5.0	1.6	3.5
Energy	3.6	3.2	4.8
Manufacture of basic metals	1.5	1.6	2.2
Accommodation and food services	1.6	1.7	2.8

Source: Statistics Iceland.

Resource-based sectors account for the majority of exports (Figure 2.2). Although natural limits to expansion are contributing to a decreasing proportion of fishing and fish processing in GDP, exports of marine products still accounted for around 39% of merchandise goods exports in 2014. The competitive position of the Icelandic fishing industry remains vital for the Icelandic economy.

Figure 2.2. **Marine products are shrinking as a share of exports**

Share of goods and services exports

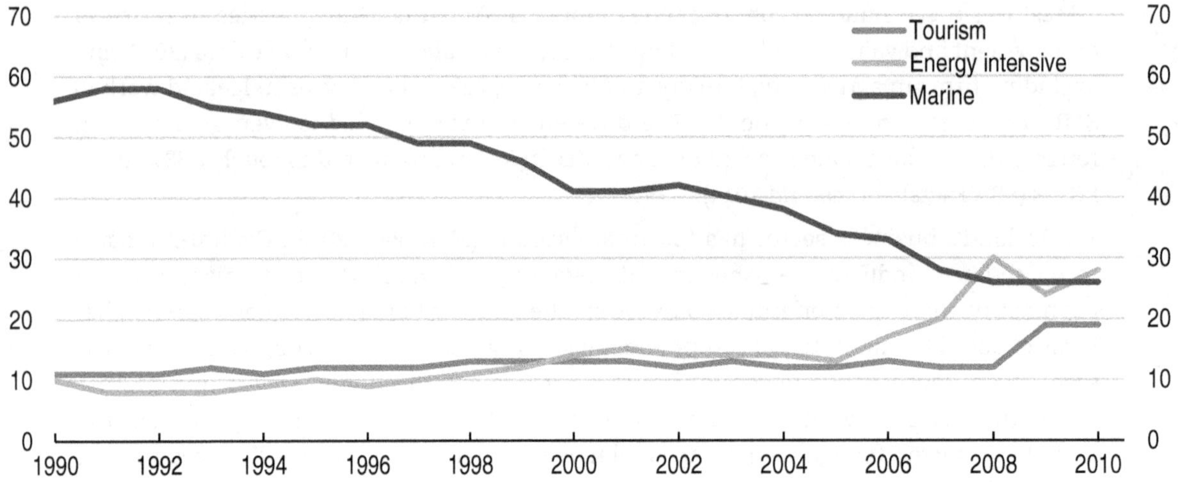

Source: Statistics Iceland

StatLink http://dx.doi.org/10.1787/888933258768

The currency devaluation following the banking crisis generally benefitted export industries such as fisheries and tourism. Since the resource base for fisheries is bounded by the biological constraints on fish stocks, the devaluation of the domestic currency increased profitability. This has led to increased investment in the fishing industry, but not an expansion of fishing activity. Expansion in the energy sector hinges upon many factors apart from the value of the króna, such as the outlook for international energy prices and prospects for additional energy-intensive projects in Iceland. There is still scope for expansion, but environmental considerations are becoming increasingly important.

The currency devaluation also boosted to tourism. Indeed, tourism can now be considered as one of the pillars of the Icelandic economy, at least based on its share in exports (Figure 2.2). From 2008 to 2014 the number of tourists arriving in Iceland nearly doubled to around one million per year, owing to the diminished cost of Iceland as a tourist destination and to other factors such as increased marketing.

The number of nights spent in Icelandic hotels has almost doubled since 2000 and the tourist season is lengthening. According to a survey of financial accounts, tourism has overtaken fisheries as a source of foreign currency revenues (Landsbankinn, 2014). The rapid growth of tourism is not only reflected in the increased share of export value, but also likely accounts for a rising share of GDP. Although Iceland's national accounts do not show tourism as a specific sector, final expenditures on hotels and restaurants have increased as a share of GDP (Table 2.1) and construction of new hotels and other tourism-related infrastructure has increased.

The main attraction of foreign tourists to Iceland is the relatively country's unspoiled natural setting. Since increased tourism itself contributes environmental pressures, the costs and benefits of increased tourism need to be assessed in order to be able to adopt appropriate policies. These may include pricing access to vulnerable natural attractions and reconsidering whether the reduced VAT rate currently in place for many tourist-related services is justified. As most tourism-related jobs require less skill and are lower-paying, there are reasons to believe that the effects of this sector's expansion on overall wellbeing may become less positive with time.

In short, although the recent boom in tourism has generated much-needed foreign exchange earnings, this potential for this sector to serve as a sustainable backbone for the Icelandic economy may be hindered by environmental issues and by its relatively low value-added. In order to secure sustainable future growth, greater emphasis needs to be given to fostering high-valued production and services through innovation and diversification.

Despite its resource dependence, Iceland has a large service sector and some strength in knowledge-based capital. Iceland compares quite well with other OECD countries with regard to R&D, both in the public and private sector. The proportion of the labour force engaged in knowledge-intensive work is high compared with other countries in the European Union and the OECD (European Union, 2014). Icelandic firms are active in innovation in such areas as medical equipment, pharmaceuticals and fishing technology. This innovation has supported the development of export-oriented manufacturing in Iceland, though most companies remain relatively small.

State-owned enterprises occupy the final sector of the economy. Although these enterprises are not numerous (around 30) they are important actors in some segments. For example, the major companies in the electricity industry are state-owned, either by the central government or groupings of municipalities. Companies investing in the industry require a license to operate and firms outside the European Economic Area are barred from direct investment.

The Icelandic taxation scheme is mixed in terms of its attractiveness to the business sector and how it promotes the efficient use of resources. The tax burden as a share of GDP is around the overall OECD average. Between 2001 and the financial crisis, corporate income taxes were relatively low at 18%, but rates subsequently were increased to 20% — closer to the OECD average of 25.5%. A capital income tax was introduced in Iceland in 1997 and is levied on various forms of payment for capital services, including interest, dividends, capital gains, and rental income. The rate applied on capital income above the personal allowance was initially set at 10% but was doubled to 20% in 2011. A value-added tax is levied on all goods and services subject to certain exemptions. While the general VAT rate is 24%, a lower rate of 11% is levied on specific goods and services, notably hotels and guesthouses. The coexistence of different VAT rates creates an uneven playing field between companies in different segments of the economy, and, other things equal, diverts resources from their most efficient uses.

Regulation is uneven

Given the small size of the Icelandic economy, the risk of market failures can be important. Although regulations are necessary to counter market failures and help to achieve specific policy aims, regulatory burdens should be kept at minimum in order to promote competition and efficiency in the economy. Iceland's overall regulatory framework for product markets is about as restrictive as to the OECD average, though some indicators of product market regulation show that barriers to entrepreneurship are relatively more restrictive (Figure 2.3).

Figure 2.3. **Product market regulation**

Indicator scale of 0-6 from least to most restrictive, 2013

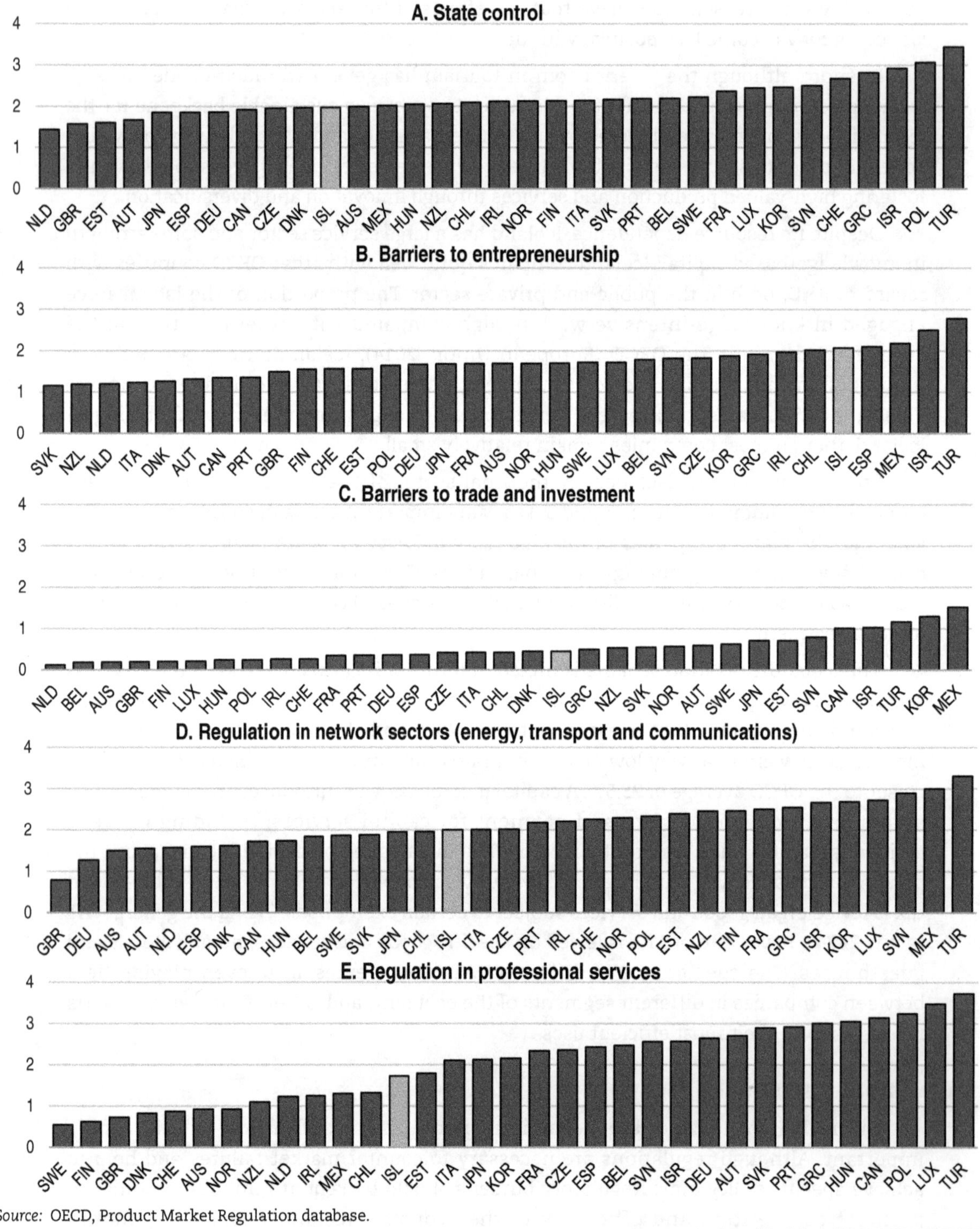

A. State control

B. Barriers to entrepreneurship

C. Barriers to trade and investment

D. Regulation in network sectors (energy, transport and communications)

E. Regulation in professional services

Source: OECD, Product Market Regulation database.

StatLink http://dx.doi.org/10.1787/888933258772

In some cases - such as retail trade, telecommunications, or land transportation - regulation is unrestrictive in comparison with the rest of the OECD. With regard to regulation of professional services, Iceland does not stand out in comparison with the OECD average. However, Iceland's regulation of professional services is elevated in comparison with other Nordic countries, whose regulatory burdens in this area are among the OECD's lowest. Given that Iceland has long had a common labour market with these other Nordic countries, this indicates room for improvement.

In other cases, often where the state maintains an interest with the presence of state-owned enterprise, regulatory burdens are more pronounced. Regulation in the electricity sector is relatively restrictive. Postal services are another area where regulation is quite restrictive, where the presence of a state-owned company ensures access in remote areas. Public policy goals of reliable and universal coverage are not incompatible with liberalising that market.

Barriers to entry

Iceland scores below the OECD average on "barriers to entrepreneurship" (Figure 2.4). This index is composed of three elements: complexity of regulatory procedures (which refers to licenses and permission systems as well as communication and simplification of rules and procedures); administrative burdens (which are measured for corporations, sole proprietor firms as well as barriers in service sectors); and regulatory protection of incumbents (which is made up of legal barriers to entry, antitrust exemptions and barriers in network sectors). While administrative restrictions on setting up a business are close to OECD averages, legal barriers are in place to prevent companies from entering specific markets and, in other cases, the licensing and permitting system is more restrictive than the OECD average. Although Iceland introduced policies that eased licensing and permitting between 1998 to 2003, there has been little change over the past decade even as reforms in many other OECD countries continued to reduce these barriers.

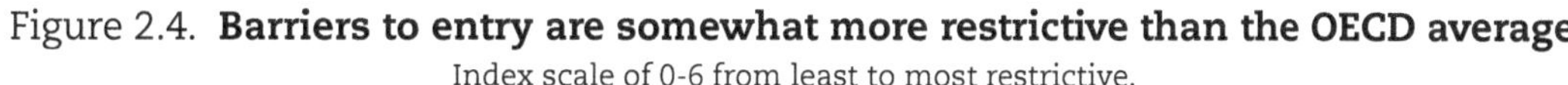

Figure 2.4. **Barriers to entry are somewhat more restrictive than the OECD average**

Index scale of 0-6 from least to most restrictive.

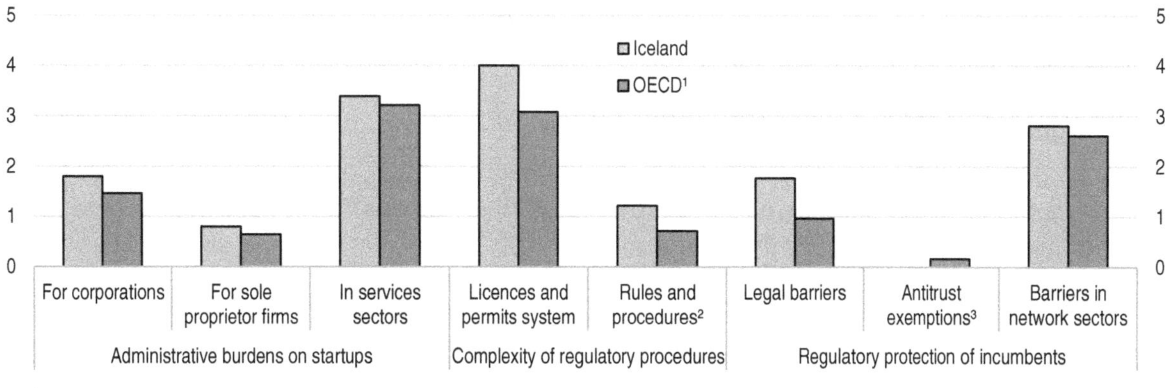

1. The OECD aggregate is an average of data available (25-30 countries depending on the year covered).
2. Communication and simplification of rules and procedures.
3. Zero for Iceland.

Source: OECD, Product Market Regulation database.

StatLink http://dx.doi.org/10.1787/888933258523

The complexity of regulatory procedures and regulatory protection of incumbents are both high in comparison with other OECD countries and Iceland's score by this measure has not changed much since 1988 despite declines elsewhere in the OECD. The administrative burden for start-ups was initially below the EU average but is now at par for corporations and is even slightly higher for sole proprietor firms. This may be a cause for concern as most start-ups in Iceland, especially in the innovative sector, are small sole proprietorships. The government should review the number of licences and permits required and simplify regulations as well as the administrative burden on establishing a business. Additional progress should be made in reviewing the legal barriers to entry in the electricity, air transport and airport, and seaport sectors. Restrictions on foreign direct investment in fisheries, where a foreign direct investment is limited to minority share holdings, are partly to blame for the high score of regulatory protection of incumbents. Limited private participation in the energy sector also contributes to this high score. The government should consider privatising the National Power Company's generation activities, which benefit from a cost-of-capital advantage conferred by government ownership, to pave the way for a competitive market in electricity generation.

As a member of the European Economic Area, Iceland is obliged to adopt EU directives on many issues that affect the ease of starting and running a business. Comparisons with other EU countries suggest that Iceland still has room for improvement, as many EU countries have successfully simplified their license and permit systems and have improved communication concerning rules and procedures. The Icelandic authorities are taking steps in this direction through increased use of on-line communications between firms and the authorities, such as establishing a one-stop website through which companies can fulfil administrative requirements. Such measures should be encouraged as they lower transaction costs and help speed administrative processes.

Foreign direct investment

Iceland does not compare favourably with other OECD countries with regards to restrictions on foreign direct investment (FDI). This is notably due to limits on foreign investments in fisheries and energy generation (OECD, 2010). Iceland's capital controls further discourage foreign investments by reducing inflows of capital, technology and know-how. Therefore, a removal of capital controls would, in the long term, help increase interest of foreign investors. Removal of other hindrances to FDI should also be put on the agenda.

Regulatory burdens should be reduced further

Reducing barriers to entrepreneurship is important for both boosting employment and productivity. Recent empirical evidence suggests that new firms contribute importantly to employment growth (Criscuolo *et al.*, 2014) and that a growing share of start-ups in a sector is associated with higher productivity growth (Adalet McGowan *et al.* 2015). The empirical evidence identifies several factors that can boost firm creation and productivity. These include high quality education, the provision of R&D subsidies to small and medium enterprises, closer R&D collaboration between business and universities, stronger patent protection, and - for more entrepreneurial firms - venture capital (Adalet McGowan *et al.* 2015). Productivity also appears to be lifted by policies directed at making firm registration less cumbersome and bankruptcy legislation less punitive for business failures. Finally, reducing the stringency of product market regulations can boost productivity in industries with high firm turnover, while reducing the stringency of employment protection legislation has a similar effect in industries with high labour turnover.

Although Icelandic governments have shown interest in improving the framework for regulatory policy and governance there is still room for improvement. Regulatory burdens are generally similar to other OECD countries on balance, but with notable exceptions. Legal regulatory restrictions, coupled with the capital controls, make Iceland less attractive for foreign investment than otherwise. *Ex ante* evaluations of the economic cost and benefits of different regulations are rare in Iceland, and in most cases estimates of the economic burden of regulations for existing businesses are not conducted as well. Proposed regulatory changes could be improved by making both *ex ante* and *ex post* evaluations of their economic costs and benefits. Strengthening the economic evaluation of regulatory policy and its framework could greatly enhance efficiency and improve the business environment.

Competition can boost productivity

One channel to boost productivity growth is through intensifying competitive pressures. Indeed, past dismantling of barriers to competition has coincided with pick-ups in productivity growth. For example, in the decade following the European Economic Area agreement in 1994, labour productivity growth averaged 2.6%, more than a full percentage point higher than its average in the preceding decade (Figure 2.5). Reforms helped raise productivity in the fishing sector significantly, in part through gains as previously inefficient firms moved towards the technological frontier. More generally, productivity in sectors exposed to foreign competition, such as energy-intensive metal production, is high compared with similar sectors in other Nordic countries, while weaker productivity in sectors sheltered from foreign competition tends to drag down the economy-wide average.

Healthy competition is generally regarded as a prerequisite for efficient market outcomes, including an efficient use of resources and sustainable growth (Ellersgaard *et al.*

Figure 2.5. **GDP per hour worked has stagnated since the crisis**

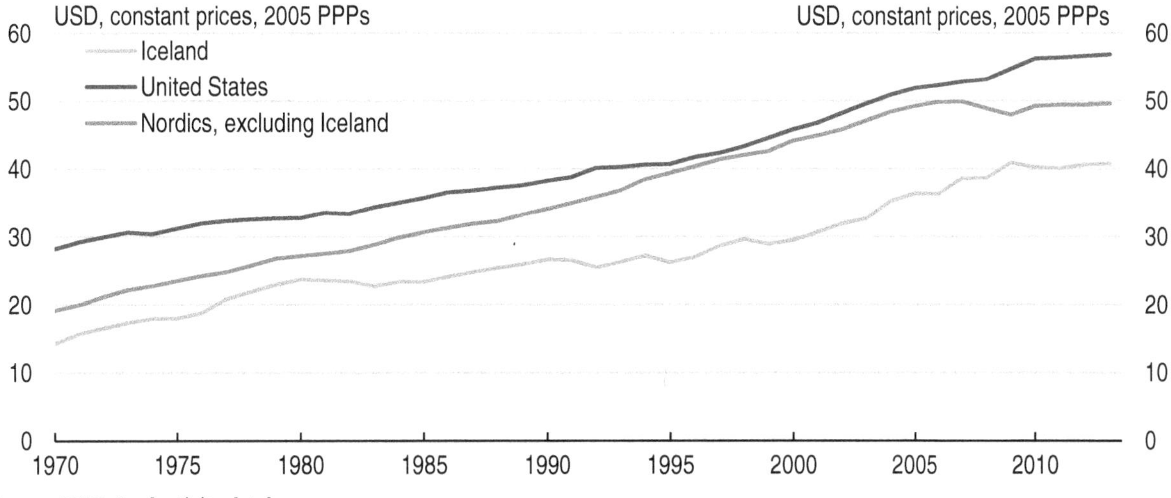

Source: OECD, Productivity database.

StatLink http://dx.doi.org/10.1787/888933258788

2013). Competition can also induce dynamic efficiency, spurring innovation and the emergence of new products and services. In what has been called the "new economy"- mostly industries and services based on advances in information technology - there are strong indications that co-operation and competition are mutually reinforcing (Evans and Hughes, 2003). Since incumbent firms in general do not profit from increased competition because it tends to diminish rents, they have incentives to stifle entry of competitors. In this light, there is role for public policy to foster competition to promote productivity and thereby lift overall wellbeing.

Achieving effective competition can be challenging in a small economy, since even modest economies of scale imply that the market can support no more than a few firms (Box 2.1). Indeed, in a number of Icelandic markets (financial, transport, telecoms, food) only a handful of companies exist or a single firm occupies a dominant position. Where a natural monopoly element is important in a given market, competition can be encouraged by separating the competitive segment and setting access rules for the monopoly segment. Iceland's competition authority repeatedly clashed with the incumbent telecom operator until 2012 before both sides reached agreement to restructure the group into separate companies for retail and wholesale operations, thereby allowing more competition to emerge in the competitive retail segment. Risks of tacit collusion and cartel behaviour can be heightened in small countries, and this has been an important concern for the Icelandic competition authorities. Over the past decade, the competition authority has concluded more than 17 major enforcement cases on abuse of dominant position and 14 major cases on cartels or tacit collusion. A number of smaller cases are not yet concluded. In light of these issues, applying the OECD's "Competition Assessment Toolkit" may be particularly helpful. The toolkit provides a means to identify pro-competitive reforms, including removing unnecessary restraints and proposing alternative less restrictive policies to achieve government objectives.

According to the *World Economic Forum World Competitiveness Index 2014-2015*, surveys of Icelandic businesses show problems related to competition, including lack of local competition and shortcomings of public policies to foster efficient competition between firms. Opening up the economy to foreign competition, either through imports of goods and services or to entry through foreign investment, would help foster healthy competition and reduce the regulatory burden of domestic competition authorities. Such liberalisation is crucial if Icelandic firms are to increase their global competitiveness and reap the benefits of increasing the share of high value-added activities in both production and services.

The Icelandic Competition Act is quite similar to EU legislation in large part because Iceland has adopted EEA Agreement articles regarding competition issues. The Competition Act establishes the Competition Authority as the competition watchdog in Iceland. Its objectives under the act include opposing unreasonable barriers and restrictions on economic activities, as well as opposing harmful oligopolies and restrictions of competition. It also grants permissions for mergers and acquisitions on a case-by-case basis where there are reasons to believe that such business transactions may have implications for competition in respective markets.

More recently, the high indebtedness of many domestic firms has made the banks important stakeholders in firms' decisions. This degree of concentration and possible conflict of interest requires careful monitoring. The slow process of restructuring, which is

Box 2.1. **Limits to public policy in a small open economy**

Given the small size of the Icelandic economy it can be difficult to enforce competition in many sectors while at the same time increasing the efficiency of the economy. This tension is recognised in the Competition Act. Economies of scale and scope in production cannot be enjoyed if market share is used as a sole measure of un-competitiveness. It has been argued that smaller markets are highly concentrated with high barriers to entry for new firms, thereby making it difficult for market forces to correct inefficient economic behaviour (Rutz, 2013).

The Icelandic Competition Authority has recognized this fact and, in some instances, has not required firms with dominant market shares to be broken apart. Rather, the Competition Authority has acknowledged the market-dominant position of such firms, which are then forbidden to use their market power to reduce competition, e.g. by applying pricing policies that restrict market entry.

It may be difficult to find the fine line between regulating market-dominant firms and diminishing potential efficiency gains from economies of scale and scope. Given this, the same competition policy should not necessarily be applied for companies that are solely operating in the domestic market and to firms that are also engaged in international competition.

An example can be drawn from Iceland's freight industry. Although there are few shipping and cargo flight firms, they compete in international markets. Competition authorities should focus their attention on checking the ease of possible entry into their market, e.g. whether lack of infrastructure creates barriers to entry. In such industries, maintaining active competition in the international market is more important than assuring competition in the local market.

In other sectors, Iceland limits both foreign and domestic competition through sector specific policies. For example, producer support for agriculture is among the highest of the OECD member countries, while fisheries are limited in their capacity to attract FDI.

Although state involvement in business operations is around the OECD average, there are still important sectors where private companies might be given a larger role to play. Notably, the energy sector is still dominated by state or municipal owned companies. By divesting the National Power Company's generation facilities, a more competitive market in electricity generation could be created. Also, the state is a large player in the postal sector, whereby a privatization of the state owned firm could increase efficiency through a more competitive market.

The OECD publishes competition law and policies indicators that measure the strength and scope of competition regimes for many countries. Iceland does not stand out in comparison with most other OECD countries by these measures. However, there is some scope for reform, especially as Iceland is one of the few OECD countries where regulation is not subject to a competition assessment (Alemani, *et al.* 2013).

reflected in the delayed rise in bankruptcy following the crisis, created uncertainty about firm ownership. The competition authorities have acted by setting limits on when companies have to be sold and by imposing conditions to ensure fair competition between companies owned by banks and other companies (such as requiring a normal rate of return and preserving the independence of the firm).

In some cases, the authorities may need to be more aggressive in pursuing competitive outcomes to support the actions of the Competition Authority. For example, complaints that the low-cost carrier Wow Air could not obtain slots at Keflavik airport that would allow it to compete with Icelandair by taking advantage of international transfers have dragged on, even though the airport's slot allocation mechanism was recognised as being detrimental to competition as early as 2008 (OECD Competition Committee, 2014). A *de facto* monopoly for domestic milk production (one dairy conglomerate accounts for almost the whole market) was partly created on the grounds that domestic producers would be in a position to compete with imports. Even so, restrictions on dairy products imports are still in force, and the competition authorities have acted against this monopolist for abusing its dominant position.

The OECD's Services Trade Restrictiveness Index shows that in a number of sectors - computing, construction, distribution, broadcasting, motion pictures, sound recording, commercial banking, insurance, road transport and courier services - restrictions are more binding than the OECD average (Figure 2.6). Restrictions on foreign entry and labour mobility were the most important factors. In part the restrictions were higher due to capital controls. This suggests that there is scope to sharpen competition through trade more generally. The introduction during 2014 of a bilateral trade agreement with China is a step in this direction. The recent step back from European Union accession need not reduce competitive pressures because the European Economic Area agreement opens borders, even if it does not cover all sectors of the economy.

Figure 2.6. **Iceland's services trade restrictiveness index by sector**

The indices take values between zero and one (the most restrictive)[1]

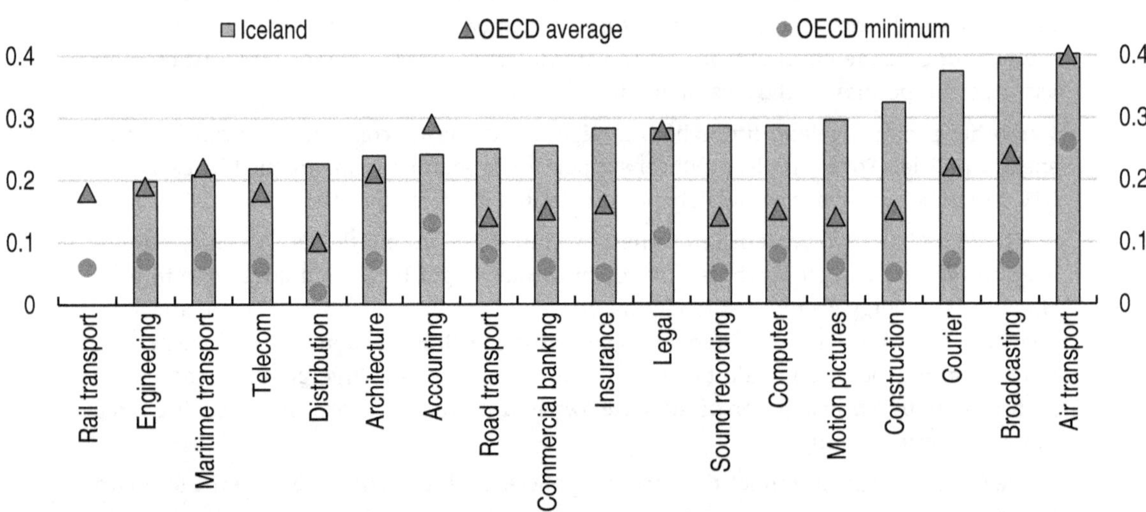

1. The index includes regulatory transparency, barriers to competition, other discriminatory measures, restrictions on movement of people and restrictions on foreign entry. The STRI methodology takes into account different market and trade cost structures across sectors to ensure that they reflect the relative restrictiveness of each sector. Nevertheless, the indices may not be perfectly comparable across sectors. The indicators are for 2013 or the most recent year available.

Source: OECD Services Trade Restrictiveness Index (STRI)

StatLink http://dx.doi.org/10.1787/888933258541

Strengthening corporate governance

Strengthening the corporate governance environment would help reinforce efficiency – as otherwise the competition authority's actions would – even in sectors where competitive pressures are weak. Empirical work suggests that robust corporate governance raises firm performance, in part by mitigating conflicts of interest between managers and stakeholders (Giroud and Mueller, 2011; Ammann et al, 2013). Iceland introduced corporate governance guidelines in 2004 and revised them in 2009. State-owned and private enterprises can be held to the same high standards of transparency, governance and efficiency, even if they pursue different objectives. However, in some cases economic efficiency appears to have been sacrificed. For example, the return on equity, after taking government guarantees into account, has been negative for the main state-owned electricity company. In part, this outcome reflects past weaknesses in decision-making within the company. Basing appointments in state-owned enterprises on professional and managerial experience should be the norm. That management is increasingly drawn from people with relevant experience is a positive sign. Furthermore, the requirement since 2014 that state-owned enterprises issue annual reports in line with the Global Reporting Initiative with the aim of promoting corporate social responsibility is also a welcomed innovation. Another potential benefit from improving the governance of state-owned enterprise arises from levelling the playing field for the private sector.

Labour and human capital influences on productivity

Labour market attachment is very strong in Iceland. Around 80% of people aged 15 to 64 in Iceland have a paid job, considerably higher than the OECD average of 65%, and particularly pronounced for women. Unemployment has traditionally been very low compared to most other OECD countries. Furthermore, the labour market is very flexible in that it deals with significant seasonal variations in employment as well as the substantial flow of workers between Iceland and other countries. During periods of strong domestic economic growth there are net inflows of labour that become more reserved as activity weakens.

One of the challenges facing the Icelandic labour market has been relatively low labour productivity growth. The average annual increase in labour productivity for the total economy since 2008 has been only 0.2%, which is among the lowest for OECD countries. Despite high participation and employment rates, there is potential to boost productivity by aiding resource reallocation and strengthening human capital.

One channel through which productivity can be lifted is through resource reallocation towards higher productivity sectors. Given the small size and open nature of the economy, facilitating the reaction to supply shocks will complement policies to support macroeconomic and financial sector stabilisation as well as boost productivity. However, a strong degree of wage compression mutes price signals as well as weakening incentives to invest in education. The distribution of income is highly compressed by international comparison when looking at differences in median disposable income by level of education (Statistics Iceland, 2015). In the past, the internal rate of return on attaining upper-secondary or tertiary education has been significantly below the OECD average. For example, estimates reported in OECD (2006) suggest that Icelandic males enjoy less than half of the rate of return experienced elsewhere. For women, the returns are comparable to elsewhere but only for those completing tertiary education. For more mobile workers, who often highly skilled, wage compression can also induce outmigration. With these effects there is a risk that the skills of available workers could erode.

Another approach to raising productivity is through increasing the skills of the labour force. Education, training, and retraining play an important role in ensuring that businesses can find people with needed skills. Unfortunately, the push of lengthy school duration and the pull of demand for low-skilled workers have contributed to high dropout rates. In Iceland, 71% of adults aged 25-64 have earned the equivalent of a high-school degree, below the OECD average of 75%. Addressing these factors to improve high-school completion rates would strengthen the skills of the labour force.

In terms of the quality of educational achievement in secondary schools, the average student scored 484 in reading literacy, maths and science in the OECD's Programme for International Student Assessment (PISA). This score is lower than the OECD average of 497. On average in Iceland, girls outperformed boys by 20 points, a wider gender gap than the OECD average of 8 points. Although Iceland does not score well on educational attainment relative to many other OECD countries, there have been improvements of late. This is reflected in the fact that the percentage of the population that has attained education below the upper secondary level has fallen from 44% in 2000 to 29% in 2011, although this level remains high in comparison with most other OECD countries (OECD, 2014). In addition, around 60% of young people in Iceland are now expected to graduate from university at some point in their lifetimes, which is the highest projection amongst OECD countries (OECD, 2014). However, Icelandic students enter tertiary education later than students in most other OECD countries, partly due to the fact that upper secondary education is usually finished relatively late (around age 20). Recently efforts have been made to lower schooling duration.

Although these are encouraging signs, there are possible challenges related to mismatches between skills and employment opportunities. After the banking crisis, the unemployment rate increased rapidly, but has since then gone down to around 4.6%. However, the composition of the unemployed has changed with the share of those with higher education qualifications rising to almost a quarter of the total number unemployed, consistent with mismatch. When the crisis hit in 2008 both Icelanders and foreign workers were affected. With the revival of economic growth there has been a marked and strong decrease in the number of unemployed Icelanders, while there has been a much less significant decrease in the unemployment rate of foreigners.

Financing remains difficult

Few Icelandic firms are listed on the stock market and most firms rely on bank loans for finance. The bank collapse of 2008 resulted in economic hardships for many Icelandic firms but bankruptcy rates have fallen back. Corporate debt as a percentage of GDP rose around the crisis but, due partly to recapitalizations and debt restructuring, has since fallen considerably to levels comparable to many other OECD countries. Interest rates have historically been higher in Iceland than in many other OECD countries. Lowering interest rates, and thereby firms' costs of capital, remains a challenge. Removing capital controls would help in this regard, both to attract outside capital as well as mitigating risks for Icelandic investors by allowing them to invest abroad.

Financing options available to Icelandic firms are similar to those in most other European countries, i.e. mainly through private financing through banks or by individual investors. The Icelandic Stock Exchange is a part of the Nasdaq OMX Exchange with 14 Icelandic firms listed. The Icelandic firms are mainly in the finance, retail, real estate, telecommunications and transport.

Interest rates

Long-term interest rates in Iceland are high compared to other Nordic countries and are only exceeded by those in Greece and Turkey amongst OECD countries. While real rates came down in the aftermath of the crisis they have ascended again of late. Compared to other European countries that were hard hit by the banking crisis, interest rates remain high. Iceland has a long history of high interest rates which reflect, *inter alia*, the risk premium associated with having a small domestic currency and the country's legacy of high inflation.

Corporate debt in Iceland was already significantly higher in Iceland than in most other European countries in the years leading up to the crisis (Figure 2.7). As the crisis hit and the banks failed, financial restructuring and writing-off debt became necessary. The decline in debt levels to a great degree came at the expense of creditors. Furthermore, the financial difficulties led to a wave of bankruptcies - especially in the years 2011 and 2012 - as many firms could not restructure their debts. A total of 7,049 firms were declared bankrupt over the period from 2008-2014. Of these, around 22% were construction companies, 18.5% were in wholesale, retail and motor vehicle repairs and almost 11% were in real estate.

Table 2.2. **Long-term interest rates in various countries**

Long-term interest rates (government bonds)	2000-07	2008-14	2014
Denmark	4.5	2.6	1.3
Finland	4.4	2.7	1.4
Greece	4.7	10.6	6.9
Iceland	8.8	7.1	6.4
Ireland	4.4	5.3	2.3
Norway	5.1	3.2	2.5
Portugal	4.5	6.4	3.8
Spain	4 4	4.4	2.7
Sweden	4.5	2.6	1.7
Euro area (15 countries)	4.4	3.5	2.0

Source: OECD Economic Outlook 97 database.

Figure 2.7. **Corporate debt mushroomed before the crisis**

Non-financial corporate liabilities (less shares and other equity), consolidated, as % of GDP

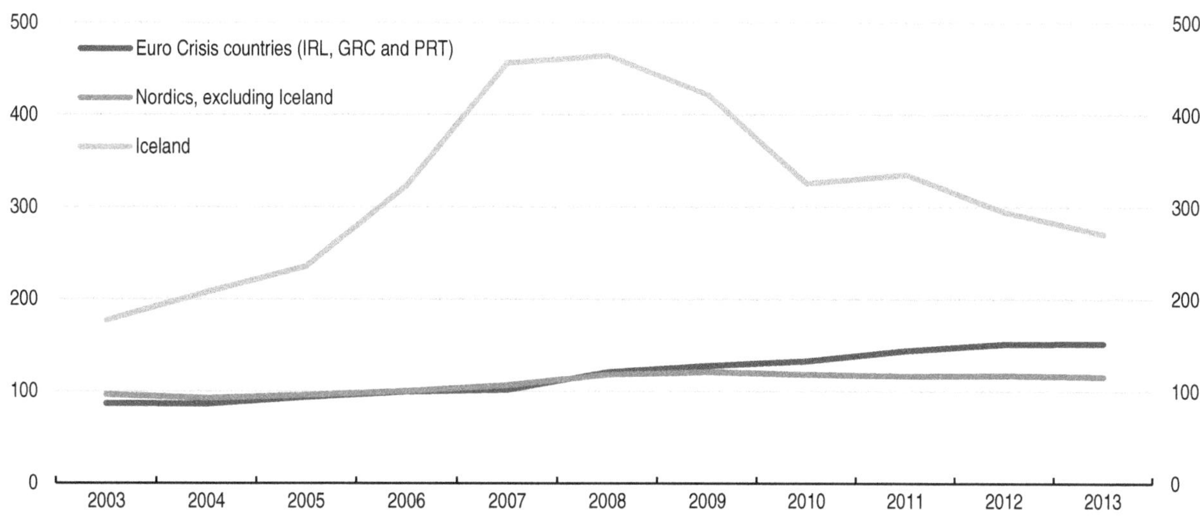

Source: OECD National Accounts

StatLink http://dx.doi.org/10.1787/888933258792

A final factor influencing financial conditions is the presence of capital controls. While the introduction of capital controls shielded Icelandic households and companies from the wake of the financial crisis, the controls have also isolated firms from international financial markets. This creates difficulties for firms seeking foreign financing and hinders them from diversifying risks by investing overseas. Capital controls also distort relative prices in the economy, leading to misallocation of resources. While it is difficult to quantify these negative effects, the longer the controls stay in place the more distortionary they are likely to become. In this context, the current plan to lift capital controls is welcome.

Public policies to foster innovation and start-ups

A good business environment increases the efficiency of established companies and should contribute to robust and sustainable growth. While established firms are engaged in innovation it is reasonable to assume that innovation will also take place in start-ups, especially in new areas of business. It is therefore important to consider whether and how the business environment encourages or discourages the start-up of new firms and entrepreneurial activities. There are various ways in which public policies can either encourage or hinder start-up as well as incentives for companies to invest in research and development connected to innovation. In our discussion we first discuss some general aspects of the Icelandic business environment concerning start-ups and innovation, including motivations for starting a business in the first place as well as the innovation activities of Icelandic firms.

Innovation activities of Icelandic firms

Innovation is not confined to producing new products or processes but is also important in services such as in marketing or organisational activities. Comparisons of innovation between different sizes of firms and different innovation activities among countries suggests that Iceland is quite similar to other countries (OECD, 2014b) (Figure 2.8). A higher percentage of SMEs are engaged in product and process innovation than in marketing or organizational innovation only. Relatively more firms are involved in both types of innovation than focusing solely on one type of activity. The percentage of SMEs engaged in innovation is similar to many other countries for which there are comparable data. In 2008-2010, the proportion of firms engaged in innovation was lower among primary producers (30%) and in the construction industry (32%) than in other industrial production (56%) and services (68%) (Rannís, 2014).

Investment in research and development in Iceland reached 42.2 billion króna in 2012 (around 2.6% of GDP), which was higher than the OECD average. Around 48% of R&D funding came from the private sector, 42% from public coffers, 2% from universities and non-profit organizations and 8% from abroad. Of public funding for research and development (mainly through RANNIS) the largest share (45%) was allocated to universities, while public institutions received around one-fourth of the funding. In 2013 funding through competition funds amounted to roughly 3.6 billion króna while tax reductions for research and development firms amounted to 1.1 billion króna.

The relatively high proportion of the Icelandic workforce engaged in knowledge-intensive work (17.5%) puts Iceland high on the ranking of OECD countries and well above the averages for the EU (13.9%), and Nordic countries (Table 2.3). In 2010, Iceland ranked third among European countries when comparing the proportion of firms engaged in

Figure 2.8. **Small firms are often innovative**

As percentage of all enterprises within that size class, 2008-10

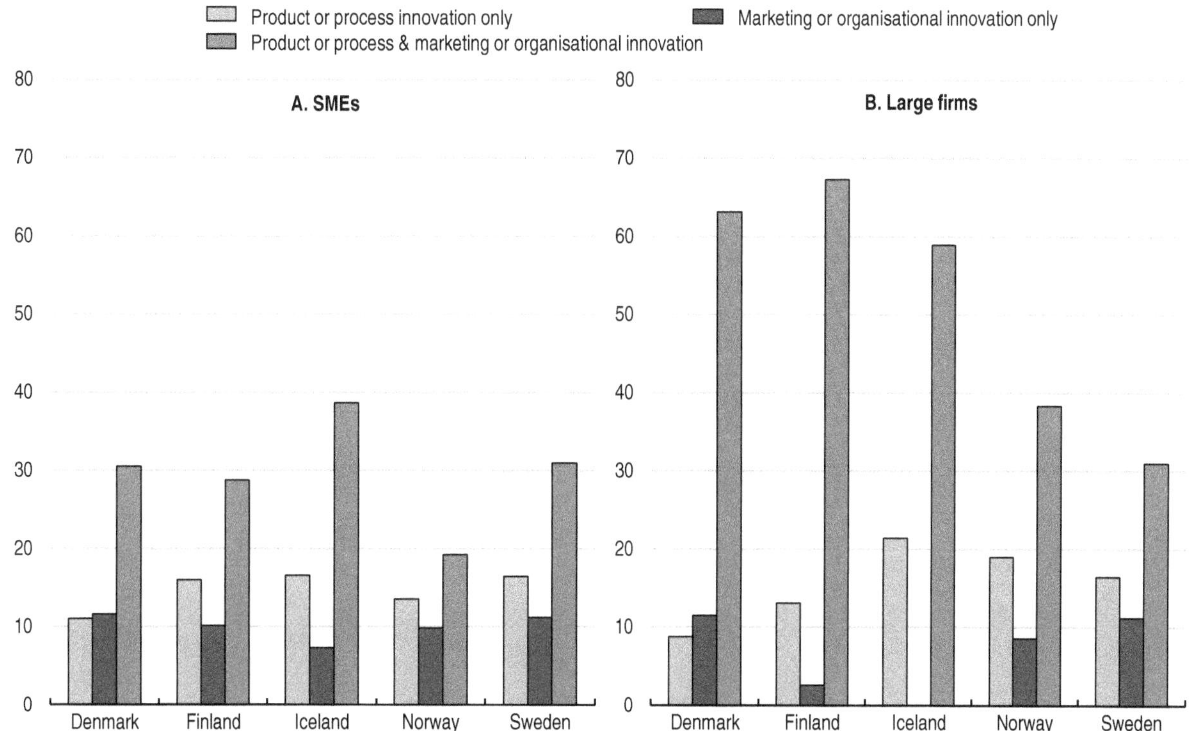

Source: OECD, Entrepreneurship at a Glance 2014

StatLink http://dx.doi.org/10.1787/888933258805

Table 2.3. **R&D activity in Nordic countries**

By employment , 2011

	Denmark	Finland	**Iceland**	Norway	Sweden
Total R&D man-years per thousand working	20.4	21.7	**19.3**	14.0	17.0
R&D man-years in firms per thousand	20.0	17.6	**12.3**	10.8	17.7
Percentage of labour force doing knowledge intensive work	15.5	15.5	**17.5**	15.3	17.6

Source: RANNIS (2014). Innovation Union Scoreboard (2014).

innovation activities (RANNIS, 2014). This emphasis on R&D and innovation is not matched by number of patent applications, measured per capita. By this measure, Iceland ranks lower than most neighbouring countries, with an average of 18.4 patent applications in the year 2009 to 2012. This may be partly explained by a relatively small high-tech manufacturing sector, where patents are of high importance.

Motivations for starting a business

There are many possible reasons for a person to start a business. According to survey data (OECD, 2014b), Iceland stands out as having the lowest percentage of respondents who claim dissatisfaction with previous work is their main motivation for starting a business. In addition, relatively few entrepreneurs in Iceland mention unmet social or ecological needs as a motivation. As in most other countries the main reason for starting a business is having a good business idea. The administrative burden of start-ups in Iceland is in the

Figure 2.9. **Administrative burdens and opportunity entrepreneurs**

Scale 0 to 6 from least to most restrictive, 2013 (2008 for United States); Percentage of all entrepreneurs, 2012

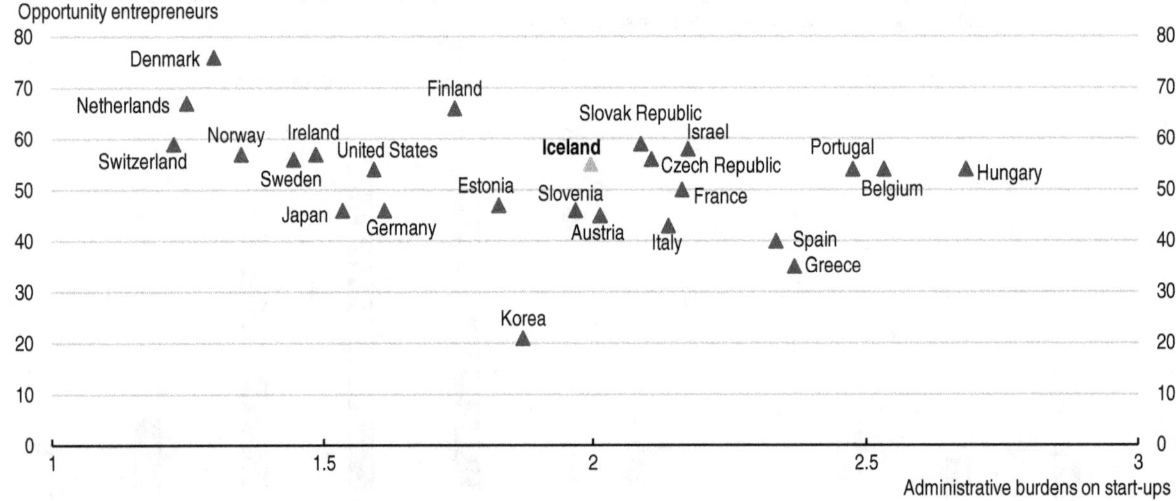

Note: Opportunity entrepreneurs are entrepreneurs who started a new business because they came across an opportunity, rather than out of necessity or by taking over a family business.
Source: OECD Entrepreneurship at a Glance, 2014

StatLink http://dx.doi.org/10.1787/888933258818

mid-range of other OECD countries while the licenses and permit system appears to be more cumbersome than in many EU-countries (SBA 2014 Fact Sheet) (Figure 2.9).

Iceland scores relatively high in public surveys about attitudes towards entrepreneurship, except for social perception of being an entrepreneur (EC, 2014). Entrepreneurs appear to have a lower social status in Iceland than in the EU, on average, and it is considered to be less of a desirable career choice. While it is relatively easy for entrepreneurs to get a second chance, measured as time to resolve insolvency and recover credits compared to many EU countries, public opinion is less supportive toward entrepreneurs that have experienced bankruptcy. This result is consistent with the relative negative perception of entrepreneurial activity in general. On the other hand, Icelandic entrepreneurs seem to have a relatively less fear of failure than many of their EU contemporaries.

Supporting firm creation and entrepreneurship

Icelandic authorities encourage innovation, research and development both directly and indirectly. The indirect support is through the public funded education system while the direct support goes mainly through two institutions: the Icelandic Centre for Research (RANNIS) and the Innovation Center Iceland. In comparison with other OECD countries, direct funding is relatively large (Figure 2.10). The Icelandic Centre for Research provides funds for R&D, generally through competitive funds for research, innovation, education and culture, as well as strategic research programmes. The Innovation Center Iceland does innovative technologic research and gives support to entrepreneurs and start-up companies. Examples of support include:

- *Action for Job Creations*, which provides grants to innovation projects as seed finance;

Figure 2.10. **Public funding of business R&D is high**

Direct public funding of business R&D, Percentage of GDP

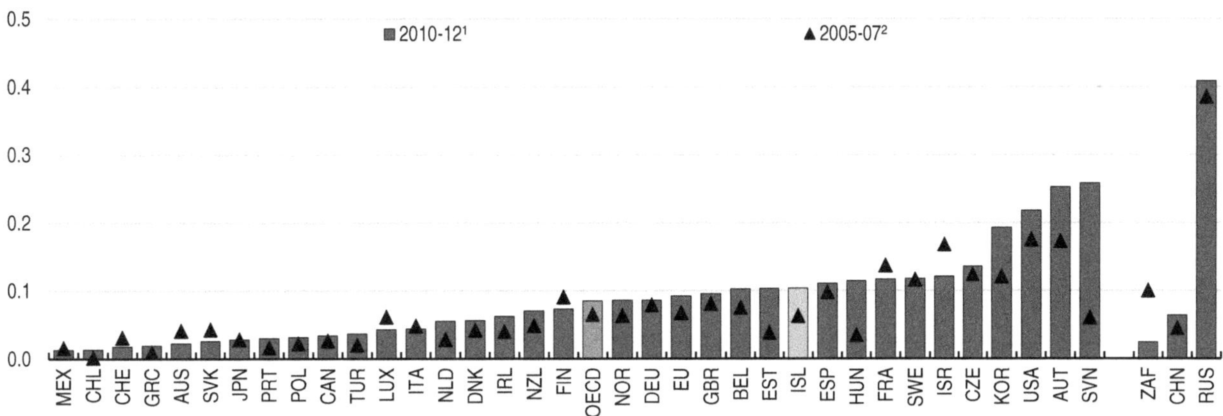

1. Average of years 2011 and 2012 for Greece; average of years 2010 and 2011 for Australia, Belgium, France, Israel, Italy, Mexico, the Netherlands, Portugal, Spain and South Africa; 2012 for Switzerland; 2011 for Austria, Iceland, New Zealand and Sweden; 2009 for Luxembourg.
2. Average of years 2006 and 2007 for Austria; average of years 2005 and 2007 for Denmark, Greece, Luxembourg, the Netherlands, New Zealand and Sweden; 2007 for Chile; 2004 for Switzerland.

Source: OECD, Science and Technology Indicators Database

StatLink http://dx.doi.org/10.1787/888933258825

- *Enterprise Investment Fund*, which is especially aimed at supporting businesses operating in Iceland outside the Reykjavik area;
- *Support to Entrepreneurs*, which focuses on SMEs outside the Reykjavik area; and
- *Step Ahead*, which subsidises consultancy costs outside the Reykjavik area.

The government has supported the creation of small firms through innovation incubators, which are often clustered to promote knowledge spillovers. Experience so far has been positive with the existing eight incubators attracting many promising entrepreneurs and links with universities being established. As this is still a relatively new initiative, the government should evaluate the effectiveness of these programs with the aim to adjust support as needed to achieve the maximum impact.

This governmental support emphasises innovation and job creation in regional Iceland. Keeping in mind that innovation itself is risky and that success of innovating firms is to a great degree dependent on possible benefits of clusters, such as deep labour markets (with regards to specialisation), specialised suppliers and knowledge spillovers (OECD, 2010), it is questionable whether support for innovation should be linked to regional policy. Such policies may reduce the success rate of innovating firms and lead to resource misallocation. Currently there exists little information on the effectiveness and success rate of the support given by the Innovation Center Iceland. Without such information it is very difficult to evaluate and design future policies. Effort should therefore be made to systematically collect, analyse and disseminate information on the effectiveness of this public support.

Tax incentives also exist to support research and innovation. Innovating firms are supported through reimbursement of research and development costs as well as tax breaks for investments in such companies. To be eligible for this support, firms have to apply to

RANNÍS to be listed as an innovating firm. To do so they have to show that they have invested more than 1½ percent of their revenues or expenses (whichever is higher) in R&D for the previous two years or that they have invested more than a specified amount in R&D over the same period. Research indicates that tax incentives for R&D benefit incumbent firms more than start-ups (Jaumotte and Pain, 2005, Westmore, 2013). Furthermore the *World Economic Forum Index on Global Competitiveness 2014-2015* underscores a below-average score with regards to the effects of taxation on the incentives to invest (97th out of 144 economies). The Icelandic authorities themselves prefer competitions for support rather than blanket tax incentives.

For Iceland, a lack of venture capital is a constraint on entrepreneurship. Partly, the lack of funds reflects the uncertainty surrounding capital controls, which will likely dissipate when the controls are lifted. High risk premia associated with macroeconomic volatility also plays a role, pointing to the need for more-effective macroeconomic stabilisation policy. Helping to establish and attract venture capital funds and other potential investors to help pool idiosyncratic risks may create opportunities to expand the investment opportunities somewhat, but the small size of the economy may limit possibilities for diversification. The government has stepped into this arena by establishing funds (one of which also involves domestic financial institutions) to promote start-ups that can compete internationally, but overall funding remains relatively modest.

A final factor contributing to barriers to entry is foreign direct investment. According to the OECD FDI Restrictiveness Index, Iceland has one of the most restrictive regimes for foreign investors. In particular, entry is severely constrained in fishing, electricity and, to a lesser extent, some parts of transportation, often through limitations on foreign equity participation. Foreign owners in the electricity sector are also limited to companies based in the European Economic Area (Sigurvaldason and Jonsson, 2010). The government is working on simplifying the legal framework for investment by non-residents in business enterprises.

Iceland seems to be performing relatively well when it comes to innovations, research and development, especially with regards to the share of firms and the proportion of the work force engaged in R&D activities. Generally, administrative burdens for start-ups are in the mid-range of OECD countries but improvements can be made in alleviating burdens related to licenses and permit systems. Efforts should be made to simplify and streamline such procedures. Access to private venture capital is still restricted due to capital controls. Furthermore, the cost of capital is high. Support to entrepreneurs should be promoted through research funds and by improving financing options rather than tax reductions that tend to favour incumbents. Also, support for innovating activities should be based on the merit of the entrepreneur involved rather than regional policy aims. Information on the success and failures of innovation projects funded with public support should be collected and analysed to help in the design and implementation of support policies.

Recommendations: Setting the course for productivity growth

Main recommendations

- Adopt an ongoing productivity agenda, including following up on the priorities identified by the recent growth forum.
- Lower barriers to entry including by removing legal barriers to entry in particular sectors.
- Support innovation, including by encouraging links with universities. Ease funding access, notably with public investment funds that can finance firm expansion. Evaluate support measures.
- Toughen competition policy implementation to ensure that abuse of dominant position or cartel/tacit collusion does not stifle competition. Use the OECD's Competition Assessment Toolkit to refine law and enforcement.

Additional recommendation

- Evaluate possible ways to reduce further the length of compulsory education and to lower drop-out rates.

References

Adalet McGowan, M. *et al.* (2015), *The Future of Productivity*, OECD Publishing, Paris.

Aghion, P., R. Blundell, R. Griffith, P. Howitt and S. Prantl, (2004), "Entry and Productivity Growth: Evidence from Microlevel Panel Data", *Journal of the European Economic Association*, 2: 265-276.

Aghion, P., and Griffith, R. (2005). *Competition and Growth. Reconciling Theory and Evidence.* The MIT Press, Cambridge, Mass. 2005.

Alemani, E., C. Klein, I. Koske, C. Vitale and I. Wanner (2013). "New Indicators of Competition Law and Policy in 2013 for OECD and non-OECD Countries", *OECD Economics Department Working Papers*, No. 1104, OECD Publishing.

Ammann, M. *et al.* (2013), "Product Market Competition, Corporate Governance and Firm Value: Evidence from the EU Area", *European Financial Management*, Vol. 19, pp. 452-469.

Arnold, J. G. Nicoletti and S. Scarpetta (2008). "Regulation, Allocative Efficiency and Productivity in OECD Countries: Industry and Firm-Level Evidence", *Economics Department Working Paper* No. 606.

Bouis, R., R. Duval and F. Murtin (2011), "The Policy and Institutional Drivers of Economic Growth across OECD and Non-OECD Economies: New Evidence from Growth Regressions", *OECD Economics Department Working Papers*, No. 843, OECD Publishing, Paris.

EC (2011). *Business Dynamics: Start-ups, Business Transfers and Bankruptcy*. European Commission. Enterprise and Industry. Bruxelles.

EC (2014a). "2014 SBA Fact Sheet – Iceland".

EC (2014b), *Research and Innovation Performance in Iceland*, European Commission Research and Innovation,

Economist Intelligence Unit (2014). "Business Environment Rankings. Which country is best to do business in?".

European Union (2013). *The Contribution of Competition Policy to Growth and the EU 2020 Strategy*. Authors, Ellersgaard Nielsen, K., S. Rolmer, F. Harhoff, S. Andersen and H. Ballebye Okholm.

Evans, L., P. Hughes (2003). "Competition policy in a small distant open economies: some lessons from the economic literature. *New Zealand Treasury Working Paper* 03/31. Wellington.

Foster, L., J. Haltiwanger., C.J. Krizan (2002). "The Link between Aggregate and Micro Productivity Growth: Evidence from Retail Trade". *NBER Working Paper Series*. National Bureau of Economic Research. Cambridge, Mass.

Gal M.S. (2001). "Size does matter: the effects market size on optimal competition policy". *Southern California Law Review*, Vol 74, pp. 1437-1478.

Giroud, X. and H. Mueller (2011), "Corporate Performance, Product Market Competition, and Equity Prices", *Journal of Finance*, Vol. 86, pp. 563-600.

IMD (2014). *World Competitiveness Yearbook 2014*. IMD World Competitiveness Center. Lausanne.

INSEAD (2013). *The Global Talent Competitiveness Index 2013*. Singapore.

Jaumotte, F. and N. Pain (2005), "Innovation in the Business Sector", *OECD Economics Department Working Papers*, No. 459, OECD Publishing, Paris.

Kalinova, B., A. Palerm and S. Thomsen (2010). "OECD´s FDI Restrictiveness Index: 2010 Update". *OECD Working Papers on International Investment*, 2010/03, OECD Publishing.

KOF (2015). KOF Index of Globalization. ETH. Zurich. *http://globalization.kof.ethz.ch/media/filer_public/2015/03/04/rankings_2015.pdf*

Landsbankinn (2014). Ferðaþjónusta. Greining Hagræðideildar. [Tourism – Economic Departement Analysis] (in Icelandic). March. Landsbankinn, Reykjavík.

McKinsey (2012). *Charting a Growth Path for Iceland*. McKinsey and Company.

Moody´s Investor Service (2014). "Credit Analysis – Iceland, Governement of." (July 15, 2014). *http://www.lanamal.is/GetAsset.ashx?id=5691*

OECD (2003). "Small economies and competition policy: a background paper". OECD Global Forum on Competition. Paris.

OECD (2010). *Cluster Policies*. OECD Publishing. Paris.

OECD (2012). *Recommendation of the Council on Regulatory Policy and Governance*. OECD Publishing. Paris.

OECD (2014a). *Education at a Glance. Country Note: Iceland.*

OECD (2014b). *Entrepreneurship at a Glance 2014*. OECD Publishing. Paris.

OECD (2015). *Economic Policy Reforms 2015. Going for Growth*. OECD Publishing. Paris.

OECD Competition Committee (2014), *Roundtable on Airline Competition, 18-19 June 2014: Note by Iceland, DAF/COMP/WD(2014)45.*

Olafsdottir, K. (2009). "Does the wage structure depend on the wage contract? A study of public sector wage contracts in Iceland". Unpublished PhD thesis. Cornell University. Ithaca, NY.

Paas, K. (2008). "Implications of the Smallness of an Economy for Merger Remedies". *Juridica International*, Vol. XV, pp. 94-103.

RANNIS (2014). "Nýsköpunarvogin 2008-2010" [Innovation Monitor 2008-2010] (in Icelandic). Rannís, Reykjavík.

Rutz, S. (2013). "Applying the Theory of Small Economies and Competition Polic: The Case of Switzerland", *Journal of Industry, Competition and Trade*, Vol. 13, pp. 255-272.

Sigurvaldason, I. and J. Jonsson (2010), "Landsvirkjun", *Mimeo*, Copenhagen Business School.

Statistics Iceland (2015), "Iceland has the smallest educational related income gap in Europe", *http://www.statice.is/Pages/444?NewsID=11774*

Westmore, B. (2013), "R&D, Patenting and Productivity: The Role of Public Policy", *OECD Economics Department Working Papers*, No. 1047, OECD, Paris.

World Bank Group (2015). "Doing Business 2015. Going Beyond Efficiency. Economy Profile 2015 - Iceland". Washington, DC.

World Economic Forum (2013). *The Global Competitiveness Report 2013-2014*. Editor K. Schwab. World Economic Forum. Geneva.

Wölf, A., I. Wanner, T. Kozluk and Giuseppe Nicoletti (2009). "Ten Years of Product Market Reform in OECD Countries – Insights from a Revised PMR Indicator". *Economics Department Working Papers*, No. 695. OECD, Paris.

ORGANISATION FOR ECONOMIC CO-OPERATION AND DEVELOPMENT

The OECD is a unique forum where governments work together to address the economic, social and environmental challenges of globalisation. The OECD is also at the forefront of efforts to understand and to help governments respond to new developments and concerns, such as corporate governance, the information economy and the challenges of an ageing population. The Organisation provides a setting where governments can compare policy experiences, seek answers to common problems, identify good practice and work to co-ordinate domestic and international policies.

The OECD member countries are: Australia, Austria, Belgium, Canada, Chile, the Czech Republic, Denmark, Estonia, Finland, France, Germany, Greece, Hungary, Iceland, Ireland, Israel, Italy, Japan, Korea, Luxembourg, Mexico, the Netherlands, New Zealand, Norway, Poland, Portugal, the Slovak Republic, Slovenia, Spain, Sweden, Switzerland, Turkey, the United Kingdom and the United States. The European Union takes part in the work of the OECD.

OECD Publishing disseminates widely the results of the Organisation's statistics gathering and research on economic, social and environmental issues, as well as the conventions, guidelines and standards agreed by its members.

OECD PUBLISHING, 2, rue André-Pascal, 75775 PARIS CEDEX 16
(10 2015 18 1 P) ISBN 978-92-64-24041-4 – 2015

www.ingramcontent.com/pod-product-compliance
Lightning Source LLC
LaVergne TN
LVHW081417110826
845149LV00010B/1767

* 9 7 8 9 2 6 4 2 4 0 4 1 4 *